My Mother's Table, The Menu, and Me

Lebanese Family Memories and Fine Foods

By Madlene Haddad Olson

Madlene Haddad Olson

My Mother's Table, The Menu, and Me
   by Madlene Haddad Olson
ISBN Number 0-9744820-0-5
©Copyright 2003   MHO Publications
                 Tel: (212) 684-6620
                 Fax: (212) 725-4709
                 Email: Info@MadlenesMarket.com
                 www.MadlenesMarket.com

Edited and published by: George Haddad
                            INET Graphics Associates
                            www.inetgraphics.com

In loving memory of

Eugenie Gebara Haddad

and

Lorraine Haddad Arida

My Mother's Table, The Menu, and Me

This book is a tribute to my mother, who together with my father, created a warm and loving family whose branches now span the entire United States. The love, values and guidance they shared with us throughout their lives have enabled us all to stay closely knit for over four generations.

It is also for my wonderful children, Edward, who enjoys cooking, and Jeannie, who I hope one day will aspire to cook. And, it is for my dear nieces and nephews, their spouses and their children - Lori, Lisa, Linda, Christie, Michelle, Teri, and Jeffrey, James, and Jay.

The book is, in fact, for anyone who may enjoy reading about a unique family history combined with a love of cooking. They might truly enjoy experiencing a little Lebanese fare along with many other delectable recipes!

It is my hope that this story and the recipes contained will follow our family line for many generations. Hopefully, our history and our recipes will be passed on to the next generation Alex, Julia, Katie, Ryan, Alyssa, Brandon, Nicole, James, Sean and all descendants of the Haddad and Gebara clan.

I do hope all of you will take as much pleasure in reading the book as I did in writing it. I know you will all make wonderful cooks – It is instinctive in a Lebanese family. Just always bear in mind – cooking is an art – paint your own dishes by altering any recipe to your taste!!

Bon Appetit!

Table Of Contents

Chapter		Page
I	Our Proud History	1
II	Coming to America	3
III	The Early Years	7
IV	The War Years	11
V	Always a White Christmas	17
VI	The Canadian Connection	19
VII	Memory Lane	21
VIII	The Family Grows	23
IX	On to Brooklyn	25
X	A Haddad Thanksgiving	28
XI	The Diplomatic Years	29
XII	School, Love and Marriage	31
XIII	Learning to Cook	34
XIV	A New Career	36
XV	My Sister and Me	38
XVI	A Weekend Retreat	40
XVII	Our Share of Sadness	42
XVIII	My Family and Me	45
	The Menu	47
	INDEX	121
	Family Photo Gallery	124

RECIPES *(The Menu)*

Food Group*   **Page**

Breakfast 49

Appetizers 53

Soup 63

Salads 67

Potatoes 73

Entrees – Middle Eastern 77

Entrees – American,Italian and other 85

Side Dishes Meatless. 99

Side Dishes Meat. 103

Middle East Desserts. 107

American Desserts 113

Miscellaneous 119

***See Index on page 121 for specific food items.**

Chapter I

Our Proud History

In our home we never referred to the "joy of cooking," but rather the art of cooking. And when you are born into and brought up in a Lebanese home, it is not simply an art or a joy but rather a gourmet's dream.

Cooking is a tremendous part of this wonderful experience. In fact, it is a large ingredient in our culture. Throughout my lifetime, My Mother's Table and The Menu have played an enormous role in our lives.

Let's begin with a brief history of my mother and father's families - the Gebara and Haddad Family - as it has been passed down through the ages beginning around 1609.

My mother's family, the Gebaras, originally came from the Kingdom of Saba in Yemen. Catastrophic floods forced them to resettle in Syria, where they established the State of Ghassanid. In the early 1600's, our ancestors were forced to leave Ghassanid after the Moslem Conquest. The six branches of the family, originally all of the Greek Orthodox faith, thereafter settled in various parts of the world. Our lineage went to Jedaidit Marjeyoun in Lebanon and many still remain there today.

The head of the family in 1609 was Prince Yusef (Joseph). The Lebanese people emulated the Ghassanids in their culture and their demeanor. They were highly intelligent, warm, loving and caring people. They have long been excellent cooks. These are still the attributes of most Lebanese people today.

It is a very nice feeling to find that the origin was so well liked and highly respected. It is indeed a bonus to all of us that we emerged from Royalty!

I have been unable to ascertain very much information about my father's family. Haddad, translated into the English language is Smith so the origins are almost impossible to know.

My grandfather, Jiddo Sam, as a young man, had come to America, with a wife, and shortly thereafter, became an American citizen. In the early 1890s, his wife passed on and in his loneliness, he returned to Lebanon. We do not know her name and there were no children from that union.

Somewhere around 1896, he went to Marjeyoun from Ain Atta, where he met my grandmothers family (Sito Takla) and asked for her hand in marriage.

She was just 12 years old, a mere child when she was promised to and married Jiddo, 25 years her senior. Sito Takla was told she would marry Jiddo Sam and she dutifully obeyed. Children simply did not question their parent's word. And in those days, daughters were secondary to sons.

They were simply born and brought up to marry, take care of their husbands and have children. There was no argument! And so, my poor grandmother left her family in Marjeyoun and returned to Ain Atta with my grandfather, where she bore her first child my Uncle Camille, at 14 years of age. James, my father, was born three years later. Imagine having and caring for a husband and two children by the ripe old age of 17!

Although just a baby herself, arranged marriages were the custom in those days and so there was nothing to say.

Chapter II

Coming to America

In 1920, Sito Takla and Jiddo Sam, immigrated to the US to start a new a new life in a strange country, across the great water, called America, with their two children Camille and Jimmy.

I sometimes think about them coming through Ellis Island in New York. I am sure it was an extremely frightening experience – but I suppose at the same time, somewhat exciting to one so young. Perhaps, in some ways they were more fortunate than others.

Since my grandfather was already an American citizen, my father and uncle could automatically choose to become American citizens, forsaking their Lebanese citizenship, which of course, they did.

Sito, having no choice, was to grow up rather quickly, and she and her sons, although missing their home in Lebanon, soon came to love America. She and the boys also became (naturalized) citizens shortly after their arrival.

Life was good in America. They settled in Clinton, Iowa. Sito was very a good mother and became an excellent cook. In fact, many of her recipes were, through the years, passed on to my mother and of course, then on to us.

Nine years after arriving in the United States, Uncle Camille met and married Aunt Josephine. My grandparents were delighted with the arrangement – after all, Josephine was a nice Lebanese girl! Like most ethnic families, in those days you more often than not – married your own kind!

A short time later, Sito and Jiddo felt that Jimmy was becoming much too wild living in the United States and it was high time he, too, should settle down with a wife! And so, with no say in the matter, at the tender age of 24, they told my father that he was going back to Lebanon with them in order to find another nice Lebanese girl for him.

It is quite laughable and almost impossible today for one to describe my father as being wild. As long as memory serves me, he was always such a gentle soul - a very quiet, kind man who worked extremely hard all his life, and was so very devoted to his family.

Upon arriving in Beirut, they visited with my mother's parents, Jiddo Farah and Sito Miriam, who was also Sito Takla's sister. Arising out of that one simple meeting, another arranged marriage ensued. After the visit, mother – also just a baby herself at 18 years old – was told she was to marry her cousin, Jimmy Haddad.

Arranged marriages were still quite common – even those to your first cousins! Jiddo Farah ruled the roost. My mother, Eugenie (Jean) was told that in three weeks, on September 23, 1932, she would marry and leave her family and home in Marjeyoun to go to America where she would subsequently spend the next 50 years of her life.

She was, as one can only imagine, totally crushed. She began to cry at the loss she would encounter. Mother had just completed her education and was planning to teach in the elementary school the same month she was told she would marry my father.

To her dismay, even her wedding gown, which in those days had to be hand made, could not be completed in time for the wedding and she was walked down the aisle wearing her older sister, Libby's, wedding gown.

Many years later, she brought out a rather large box that had been carefully packed away. As she opened the box to show Lorraine and me the contents, we looked at it with awe.

It was a lovely white silk-and-lace bridal gown that had been created for her wedding - and we fell in love with it!

Alas, the beautiful gown was never put to use, the fabric was so delicate that even as we tried it on, the lovely dress began to disintegrate.

My father, once again came through Ellis Island to this new world – but this time with a new young wife who spoke little English and who would leave her family, not to see them again for 27 years.

When she finally returned to Beirut for a visit those many years later - where most of her family now live - there were huge celebrations in her honor. And when she went to revisit Marjeyoun, people came from miles around to greet her. It was indeed a joyful time for my mother and for all of her family.

After returning from her first trip, she brought back a lovely painting of her Family Tree, which one of her cousins, Fares Gebara, had researched and hand painted. In fact, today the tree still stands proudly on the Merjayoun.net/Gebara Website.

It was not just beautiful but absolutely fascinating for all of us to see. Unfortunately, the names are all written in Arabic so we are unable to match the exact order of the relatives. My mother did, however, point us out and I know we are towards the end on the right hand side of the tree.

An interesting point in the family history, is that my mother's uncle, who was also her godfather, was one of the passengers on the Titanic. We never learned too much about the trip and only knew that he was one of the lucky survivors. He subsequently went back to Lebanon, never to return to the United States.

After we grew up, Mom returned to Lebanon a few times, sometimes with Dad, and as the years passed, they always had a wonderful time. Three of her full sisters –Libby, Nozick and Georgette – all came to America and spent some time with us. Only Aunt Yvonne, has never been here. We loved meeting our relatives and eventually we were able to meet many of their children, some of whom immigrated or visited the United States through the years.

So many of our first cousins passed through New York and spent some time visiting with us. A few of them even came to live with us while they completed their education in New York.

Apart from Mom and Dad, the only person in our immediate family who was fortunate enough to visit Lebanon is my brother Rick. He went as a young man and was utterly taken in by the beauty of Beirut and all of our relatives. He was adored and doted on by everyone. It was a wonderful experience that I know he will never forget.

So many times through the years, Lorraine and I talked about and planned to fly to Beirut, but unfortunately, there was always something to stop us. Initially, we could not afford it, then the kids were too young or someone had just died or the war was going on. Sadly, the trip never came to be.

I shall always regret not having the opportunity to visit and to know all of my relatives and the beautiful country. It seems with certain things in life, the moment always passes. Apart from meeting all my wonderful relatives, I would dearly have loved to have seen the snow-capped mountains combined with the lovely white beaches with Lorraine.

And yet, I have not given up the hope that someday, the Good Lord willing, I will eventually find my way to visit Lebanon.

Chapter III

The Early Years

Near the end of the great depression Mom and Dad, after arriving in America, went on to Clinton, Iowa where Dad's parents had settled. Mother was so very lonely in those early years, living in a new country away from her entire family. However, she always had a very strong constitution and quickly learned to adjust to this new world. She bore three children during the first four years she arrived in the US.

Lorraine, George and I were all born during that time - Jimmy and Ricky were still just a gleam in my parent's eye. The end of the depression was not even a memory for us, and of course, the Second World War was just a blur.

While pregnant with George, Dr. Broomer reprimanded Mom and told her she had no business having so many children in such difficult times. She was acutely embarrassed but had no response - she knew nothing of birth control and just hung her head in shame!

Many years later, while reading the newspaper in Brooklyn, she read that Doctor Broomer's young wife had given just his him first child, a son, at the age of 90! She thought this was so funny and she certainly had a good laugh at this news that traveled from Clinton, Iowa to Brooklyn, New York!!

Shortly after the three of us were born, and although the depression was allegedly over, my father was forced to leave the family with his parents in order to find work in Davenport, Iowa. He worked in a restaurant as a short order cook and earned just $10 per week. He ate his meals at the restaurant and paid $5 a week for his room. He sent the other $5 home to support my mother and the family. It was indeed fortunate that we lived with his parents at that time.

Although those early years were fine for the children, they were difficult years for my parents, particularly for my mother. Jiddo Sam was not the easiest person to live with and although they had a washing machine, Mom was never allowed to use it and had to wash all of our clothes by hand using a scrub board!

Sito did most all of the cooking, but my mother helped and she always watched my grandmother prepare the meals, **Baking Bread, making Meat Pies, Spinach Pies, Lamb Stew, Roast Chicken** and many other Middle East dishes.

Although from the beginning, he gave my mother a difficult time my grandfather did, however, love his grandchildren and was always so very good to us.

After a few years, we moved into our own home right next door to Jiddo and Sito and I can vividly recall many a time going to their home for breakfast. We would sit in awe watching my grandfather eat a dozen eggs for breakfast with mounds of toast slathered in jam!

He would then sit us on his knee, bend over and scratch our faces with his beard. We would giggle with joy and we just loved him. I was only six when he left us – but the memories lingered on.

Ironically, the year prior to his death, Jiddo had a complete change of heart. By that time, he felt Mom was really a very good person and decided she was worthy of the family. At that point, he could not do enough for her. He gave her almost anything she wanted – including the use of the clothes washer!

Jiddo Sam lived to be lived to be 85 years old so one can only believe that in some instances, eggs were quite good for you.

Many a day, Sito would gather us around the table and tell us stories that were handed down through the years.

One of our warm favorites was that of my Mother's grandfather, whom we were told was a very religious man. He was walking home through the woods, on a dark rainy night, in Lebanon. In the denseness of the forest, he had lost has way home and began praying to St. Peter to help him.

As he trudged through the woods, suddenly the sky lit up and, low and behold, he saw a rather large man in a white robe. He had a set of keys hanging from his waist and my great grandfather instinctively knew that this had to be St. Peter, holding the keys to the Kingdom. What a glorious sight for him.

St. Peter said to him, "Do not be afraid", and went on to say, "because you are such a good person, I will grant you just one wish." My great-grandfather asked only for long healthy lives for all of his children. The youngest of his eight children lived to be 86 years old and he died that young simply because he accidentally stepped in front of a car while crossing the street!

Another favorite tale took place on January 5, the night of the Epiphany, when the entire town would go to the river to emulate the baptism of our Lord. They would hang their clothes on the bushes at the bank of the river and would bathe in the river at the stroke of midnight.

When the townspeople came out of the water, to their shock, they found that most of their clothes were stolen on this very holy night. The next morning they returned to search for them and to their complete amazement, as they neared the river, they looked up and saw their clothes hanging from the tops of the trees.

It is believed that on that most Holy Night of the Epiphany, the trees were bowing to our Lord. This story, of course, can never be proven but then, no one can really say that it was fiction.

In our home only my father spoke fluent English — mother knew some English and French, but she always spoke to us in Arabic. By the time Lorraine started school, Lorraine, George and I, only spoke Arabic. At that point it became quickly apparent that not only did the children have to learn the English language, but so too, did my mother.

Many years later, I recall a friend asked me what kind of accent my mother had. Totally taken by surprise, I blankly looked at her indignantly and replied, "My mother does not have an accent!" The funny part is, she believed me.

Chapter IV

The War Years

After the start of World War II, our lives financially took a complete reversal. My father had returned from Davenport and was working at John Hancock Insurance Company. I remember seeing my mother looking so sad and with many voluntary and involuntary tears coming from her eyes, as she listened to the radio declaring the news that the Japanese had bombed Pearl Harbor.

My father came home from work that evening and immediately announced to my mother that he was going to join the Army. With that, she cried even more- and we cried with her – far too young to really understand why!

Sadly for my father, but happy for the rest of the family, he was told that he had flat feet, was too old and had too many children to go into the armed forces and they were sorry but he should look for other ways to serve his country.

Uncle Camille, at the time, was working as a chef and my father was still selling insurance for John Hancock. They decided the best way they could serve the country was to open a restaurant and serve the people of the town and the visitors. And so, they purchased the Mae Alden Café and subsequently they turned it into the very best restaurant in town.

There was an Army hospital in town as well as an Italian prisoner of war camp. Clinton was simply inundated with soldiers and their families – always looking for a good place to eat when they came to visit their husbands or children.

My uncle had now become a fabulous cook and my father managed and hosted the restaurant. Although Dad was a good cook and did some cooking, Uncle Camille was truly the gourmet chef.

During those years, the restaurant grew and prospered. Jimmy and Jean and Camille and Josephine, were working very hard and more than doing their part to feed and give some comfort and solace to the troops and their families during wartime.

Our home and restaurant became home away from home for many soldiers and their families. Soldiers came to our house for breakfast, lunch and dinner on any given day and many would bring their wives and even their children. My parents happily gave up their bedroom for them and gave them much joy by sharing our life with them.

The soldiers and my parents found many lasting friendships during those years. Long lines of people came from miles away and waited around the block for hours to taste the delicious fare the restaurant had to offer. The soldiers that came to the restaurant on their own were always given a special rate on anything they might order. No serviceman ever paid more than $1 for a full course meal. The restaurant was known throughout the area and it was during those years that "My mother's Table" became a gourmet's feast.

The restaurant was closed one day a week on Wednesday, and although we had rationing, there was always an abundance of food for everyone who came to our home. It was wartime but somehow the food was plentiful and we fed many a soldier and their families. On any Wednesday, mounds of them automatically arrived at our doorstep for lunch and/or dinner or just to say hello.

Nearly every day mother would create a feast! Her table always included such delectable items as **Roasted or Fried Chicken, Looby and Rice, Kibbee, Meat Pies, Hummus, Baba Ghanoush, Kefta, and Koosa, Stuffed Eggplant and Rice.** The servicemen and their families could never get enough of her wonderful food and many a wife constantly asked for her recipes.

As I think back, My Mother's Table was like a gourmet restaurant, primarily, I believe because she was always able to stretch the delicious fare to feed as many people that came to visit. She served mostly Middle Eastern food like **Malfoof** (Cabbage Rolls), **Grape Leaves**, and **Koosa** that did not require a great deal of meat – and we always ate pita bread with our meals. With an absolute certainty, this explains our girth today!

Little did we understand what our parents meant when they said, "You must eat all the food on your plate - the children in Europe are starving." Food was never wasted and bread was never thrown away. We were brought up with the thought that bread was the staff of life and even stale bread was used for dishes like **Fatoosh**, a delectable salad, or **Bread Dressing for Chicken or Turkey**. To this day, I simply cannot throw away bread. Many a day, the birds and my dogs are so very happy to get the leftovers.

Most Sunday afternoons all of the children were sent to the movies so Mom and Aunt Jo could help out in the restaurant. We were each given 10 cents to get into the theater and 10 cents for popcorn.

If a second film was playing that we wanted to see, we would skip the popcorn and since two of the three theatres in town were next door to each other, we would remain to see the second film and forfeit the popcorn.

We were not allowed in the restaurant early in the afternoon on Sundays, because of the great throngs of crowds, but after the movie, we went directly to the restaurant that was around the corner from the theatres. We headed straight to the kitchen and were all allowed to have our dinner. It was such a wonderful treat.

Our favorite choice was the **Prime Ribs of Beef.** It was served to us in slivers and it wasn't until years later that I learned that Prime Ribs was normally served as a slab of beef!

The food was among the best food we ever tasted – we had never really eaten American food until the restaurant opened, so we were exposed to the delicious American cuisine of my Uncle – some of which included **Beef Stew, Pot Roast, Baked Steak, Virginia Ham Chili, Spaghetti and Meatballs** and so many other wonderful meals.

The war, of course, was not real to us – we were simply too young. It only meant that we would have air raids in school and would sit on the floor in the halls, with our hands wrapped around our heads. Sometimes late in the evening, we would have blackouts. All the lights would go out and we would sit in awe and watch the beams of light fly across the sky against the total darkness.

The war also meant that on those very rare occasions, the family could share a steak dinner. It was usually a **Chuck Steak** and my parents always served the children first for such a delicious dinner. I remember the two of them sharing just a small piece with the fat and bones, so that the children could really enjoy the meal. My mother and father were quite possibly, the kindest and most generous people I have ever known!

I also remember that at those very infrequent times, bubble gum was available in the local candy shop. The shop owners, trying to be fair to all, would allow us to buy just two pieces of gum for three cents. Since we usually had money, we would sometimes send a friend to the store to buy an additional two pieces of gum and one was given as a reward to that friend!

We were far too young to realize the horrendous affect of the war on the world. Life for the children, was happy and fun. Lorraine and I took piano lessons, tap dancing and ballet lessons every week and of course, both of us were Brownie and Girl Scouts and George was a Cub Scout and later a Boy Scout.

As I think back, it puts a big smile on my face to think of Lorraine and I dancing on our toes! We thought we were so lovely! As the years passed, Lorraine continued to play the piano more or less as a hobby. The only tune I can still play is Happy Birthday! So very often I wish I had continued on with the music.

George, as the only boy for six years, was, as one might imagine, doted upon and spoiled but he was always the little gentleman. Although so young, I vividly recall the Italian prisoners of war who were brought to the schoolyard across from our house to exercise and play soccer. Many of them would pick George up, hug and kiss him and cry as they remembered their own sons in far away Italy!

It was a poignant and bittersweet sight to see our American soldiers carrying guns guarding these poor wretched Italian prisoners, who really wanted nothing but to return home to Italy to their families.

Initially my mother was a bit frightened and one day she asked one of the guards if the prisoners were very dangerous. He laughed and told here they were as gentle as could be and they were only guarded with guns, because the soldiers were instructed to do so.

One time, three of the prisoners did escape, but they had no place to go and they were finally found hiding in the closet of someone's house. Where on earth could three Italian prisoners who spoke no English hide in a place as remote as Clinton Iowa? I think they were probably so frightened and happy to get back to the camp.

Many of our weekends were spent visiting with a family who we called "Uncle John and Aunt Rose" on their farm outside of Clinton. We learned in those days that not everyone's life was always as easy or wonderful as ours. The farm was fairly run down – and they still used a wood burning stove for cooking and for heat.

The worst part for us was that they had no lavatory - everyone had to use the outhouse! This of course, did not sit well with us — but then again - when you have no choice … They were, however, always so happy to see us and welcomed us with open arms - and we loved them.

We fed the chickens, the sheep and the pigs and learned to milk the cows. We dug up potatoes and fresh carrots and picked corn for lunch. We gathered eggs from the chicken coops and played hide and seek running in and out of the cornfields.

It was, indeed, a wonderful experience and my only regret is that my children, Edward and Jean, and indeed, all my nieces and nephews, were never given the opportunity to experience this kind of life. What a delight it was to grow up in this environment!

Our dinners at the farm almost always consisted of fresh killed **Roasted Chicken, Hashwi (Rice and Meat Stuffing), Corn on the Cob and either fresh vegetables, Tabooli or Mixed Salad.**

We always returned home, happy and content, and looking forward to the next visit to "The Farm."

Chapter V

Always a White Christmas

C hristmas was so very special an occasion as we were growing up. The entire family – in fact, everyone in town went caroling from house to house and we all went walking through the glistening snow to visit the Eiten Home that was at the top of our street.

Each Christmas the house and the great sprawling lawn were covered with live camels, sheep, donkeys and life-size figures of Mary, Joseph and the Little Lord Jesus adorned the stable. A life-sized Santa Claus together with the eight reindeer covered the entire length of the top of the house.

Rudolf had not yet emerged – but the beautiful carols – *Silent Night, O Come All Ye Faithful, Away in a Manger, Hark the Herald Angels Sing, The First Noel*, and all of the traditional carols rang out all through the night for many weeks.

The soft snow falling on the lawns was so white and clean. We almost always had a white Christmas in Iowa and it seems like the snow never changed from its silvery white powder.

Each child in those days received just one gift from Santa and I can still recall my all-time favorite gift. It was what I believed to be the most beautiful doll I had ever seen. She was a "Miss America" doll that was about 12 inches tall and it was adorned in a long white satin gown with a royal blue jacket and a blue army hat with gold and red trim. I was bursting with love for her and felt that I would never again receive such a wonderful gift.

Much to my sheer disillusionment, I found the doll two nights *before* Christmas, and that was the last time that I went to bed on Christmas Eve with thoughts of Santa Claus coming through the chimney.

From that day forward, although I knew the answer –
no matter how many times I questioned her - my mother always said, "Santa exists if you believe in him."   I think
these were very wise words, indeed, and I have always
passed these words on to my own children.

I love Christmas and have always enjoyed the day with
my family, but I must say that today I still remember that
doll like it was yesterday. It must have been one of the
more memorable Christmases in my life.

Our Christmas dinners were as one might imagine, always a feast. We inevitably served **Turkey and Dress-
ings, with Mashed Potatoes, Sweet Potatoes, and
every conceivable accompaniment with a multitude
of trimmings** and there was both Arabic and American
food and most always a houseful of company!

It was definitely the most wonderful and happy time of
the year. My parents invited so many servicemen to our
home and made them feel that they were all at home for
Christmas.

It was indeed a wonderful and thankful time not only
for our family, but for all of the people whose lives were
touched by my parents and their love and generosity.

Chapter VI

The Canadian Connection

Most of our early summers were spent in Canada visiting with relatives in Montreal and my parents always rented a summer place in the Laurentian Mountains.

Each June when school was finished, mother and the three children would ride the train to Montreal. It was great fun for us. Our rented house in Ste. Adele was at the foot of "Cross Mountain."

Sometimes we would ride the train, which was an overnight trip, with my mother and other times we would drive to Canada with my father. When we took the train, Dad would usually join us for the last two weeks of the summer for his holiday - just in time to drive us back home.

Many of our relatives lived in Montreal and on any given weekend, we had an enormous number of people at the house picnicking on a feast prepared by Mom, Sito Takla and her Sisters, Aunt Katrina and Aunt Rose.

During one of our visits my mother, Sito Takla and my aunts decided they were going to cook a "special" garlic dinner. It was a disaster and the strong odor of garlic permeated the entire town of Ste. Adele for several days. Neither we, nor the townspeople were exactly pleased with this. Needless to add, this meal was never cooked or mentioned again until now.

One summer in Ste. Adele, our cousins and us (it was Larrry, Bea, Kenny, Lorraine, George and I – Jimmy, Ricky, the additions to our family and Elaine in Uncle Camille and Aunt Jo's came along about seven years later) decided to climb the mountain to see the cross at the top.

Of course, we could have taken the very simple way that was to go up the ski path and down the same way, but we all decided it would be such fun to come down the mountain through the woods. And it was fun initially – and then, the unthinkable happened. All of us were lost in the forest!

We found a huge rock at a clearing and could see our house at the bottom of the mountain. It appeared to be so close, as though we could jump down off the rock and walk home quite easily. We decided against this and decided to walk around the rock because Kenny had previously hurt his leg and we were fearful that he would further injure it.

This was a sheer stroke of luck, because by the time we got down the mountain, we found it was actually not a rock but a huge cliff and we would have all been killed. What we saw was the tops of the trees in the forest and thought it was the ground. God was surely watching over us.

Chapter VII
Memory Lane

There are so many memories connected with those years. Lorraine was the oldest and also the strongest and George and I were always competing against Lorraine. One day while we were playing a game in Canada, we really showed her, she swung me around and I fell and broke my arm!

No one knew that the arm was broken until the next day when it was swollen and I had to go to the hospital to have it set! My mother and father were certainly not too happy as they took me to the hospital – and neither was I!

When the war finally ended – Lorraine, George, and I were so excited because we were told that Dad would drive us around town to throw paper confetti out the window in celebration of this joyous event.

We had such a good time that when we returned home, we shredded every newspaper we could find, believing we would be going out the next day and do the same. What a disappointment to learn the end of the war meant the celebration of throwing confetti was done for just one day.

The three of us did almost everything together, including being sick or incapacitated. We even all had our tonsils removed together. What a horror that was.

I remember it like it was yesterday. The three of us were kept in one room. I was about three years old and in a crib when they took Lorraine away and wheeled her back into the room sound asleep with blood trickling from her mouth.

My first thought was that she was dead and they were going to kill me. I started screaming and holding on for dear life to the sides of the crib.

But I lost the fight and was forced to have my tonsils removed! Apparently I was allergic to ether and swallowed my tongue three times!

I can't think of a single good thing that came of that episode – except, although we all had a sore throat, we were allowed ice cream every day!

The three of us always got sick together. Whether in Canada or in Clinton, measles, mumps, colds or flu or what have you – came to all of us at the same time. Mom really had her hands full when we were well, so it must have been total agony for her when we were sick. But she never really complained.

Chapter VIII

The Family Grows

Seven years after George was born, my mother again found she was having a baby. The excitement following Jimmy's (Junior's) birth – on my mother's birthday - was fantastic and as one would expect, he was the pride and joy of the entire family. It was one of the waitresses in the restaurant that coined the name "Junior." From day one as soon as my mother would arrive in the restaurant, Peggy would ask "How is Junior?" The name stuck with him for most of his life.

He was adored not just by all of us but the entire staff at the restaurant doted on him. We loved him dearly and pampered him as much as any big brothers and sisters could. His complexion was somewhat darker than the rest of us – he looked very much like my father and when he tanned, he was extremely dark.

By the time Jimmy was three years old, the war was over and mother wanted to live near her relatives who had settled in Montreal and New York. It was a difficult decision for my parents to make so they decided we would spend six months in Montreal to see how we would like living there and if Dad could find suitable work.

And so, we started school and began really getting into learning to speak Canadian French. After six months we quickly discovered that our French was not really up to par. We were delighted to hear that my parents decided Montreal was not the place they wanted to live and it was then that the decision was made to move the family to New York.

Our New York relatives included two of my mother's half brothers Aref and Sam, and one half sister, Zakia. Many of her family – in fact, all of her full sisters and only full brother, Libby, Nozick, Georgette, Yvonne and Alif - were still in Lebanon. Today, with the exception of Aunt

Libby and Uncle Alif who have passed on, they still remain there.

There were around 16 children in her family. Jiddo Farah's first wife had died and he married my grand-mother, Sito Miriam who was a widow with one son, George, who faced an untimely death at the age of 33.

Jiddo Farah was born in 1856 and his last child was born when he was 72 years old. As far as we are aware, he left this earth around 1939.

I was just a young child but I recall my mother and Sito Takla crying over the news of Jiddo Farah's death. We had drapes over our doorways rather than doors and I wrapped myself in the drape and started crying just because they were. I think it must have been my first memory.

Chapter IX

On to Brooklyn

And so, the restaurant was sold and Uncle Camille's family moved to Arizona and we moved to Brooklyn, New York in September of 1946. It was so exciting. We had no furniture and our house was not quite ready when we arrived but I remember driving up a beautiful tree lined street across from a park, with my family, as we stopped in front of our new home.

We spent the first few weeks living at Uncle Sam and Aunt Olga's home. Lorraine and I shared beds with our cousins Delores and Claudie, and George and Jimmy slept on the floor – but it was a fun time as we waited to move into our new home.

I fell in love with New York and with our beautiful house that reminded everyone of a castle. My love of the house was so great that even after my parents left us for a better place, I bought the house from my sister and brothers, and we lived there until Ed and I finally decided to sell it in 1997 and moved the family to New Jersey to be near Lorraine and her family.

After we arrived in New York, Mom once again found she was with child and Rick joined us the following January. He was a darling baby and we all loved him dearly. There was just one problem. We had just three bedrooms.

Jiddo Sam had passed on and Sito Takla was living with us for six months out of the year and at Uncle Camille's home the other six months. She was sleeping on a pull-out couch in the dining room and since the bedrooms were full - Rick spent the first six years of his life in a crib in my parents' room!

One fine summer day the entire family went to the beach in Coney Island. We all were having such a good time playing in the sand and swimming in the ocean – until we discovered that Junior, who was around four or five years old by then, was missing.

We became frantic and searched high and low for him fearing the worst. My poor mother and, of course, the rest of us panicked. He was not with the lost-and-found children! In those days, black and white children were separated and low and behold, we finally found Jimmy with the black children calmly sitting on a bench waiting for us to collect him!

Rick, who was the baby in the family, was a delightfully happy baby who always had a smile on his face and just loved to eat – no matter what was put before him. Actually, both he and I are still that way today.

One night my mother prepared a meal she had never made before. I can't even remember what it was called and please be assured, it will not be included among my recipes. It was made with rice and onions, covered in pomagrantz seeds, yogurt, lamb, pignolia nuts, and what have you.

None of us were allowed to leave the table until our plates were clean. Rick was still a baby in a high chair. Mom and Dad, weary of waiting for us to finish, left the table and told us not to leave until our food was finished. We looked at Rick, who was the only one among us who was truly enjoying his food.

The idea then came to us that we should at least give part of our food to Rick – and so, one by one, we gave him a mouthful from our plate. We were at the table for about two hours – but Rick did well by all of us. He ate every drop of food on our plates. Mother was so pleased that we all cleaned our plates – until Rick burped! Needless to say, we were all punished.

As much as Rick loved food – Jimmy, on the other hand, did not like meat in any way shape or form. Even as he matured, he always favored meatless meals. As a little boy, he would more often than not, sneak his portion of meat from his plate and hide it under the refrigerator.

He thought he was so clever, until one day, mother discovered a horrible odor in the kitchen. She looked everywhere to discover where it was coming from. Finally, she could no longer stand it – and literally tore the kitchen apart to find where the foul smell was coming from.

Lo and behold, she finally removed the bottom shelf off the refrigerator and found the mounds of food Jimmy had stored away. Following that episode, one of us always sat at the table until Junior finished his dinner.

It was really a wonderful life and by then mother was an acclaimed cook and we had relatives and friends at the house nearly every weekend. Her family, both in New York and in Beirut, was very large. Our house was always like Grand Central Station on any given weekend.

Uncle Sam and Aunt Olga and their family, Delores, Claudia and their brother, Paul Jabara would frequently come to the house and Paul would entertain us with song and dance.

Paul went on to become a huge success and won an Academy Award for the song "Last Dance." He wrote many great hits for stars like Donna Sommers, Barbara Streisand and many others. Unfortunately, he was taken from us at the young age of 42, but his memory and his music still live on.

Chapter X

A Haddad Thanksgiving

Thanksgiving was always one of the most memorable occasions in our family, and it was always spent at my mother's house.

As a baby, George had developed pneumonia around Thanksgiving and my mother made a vow that if George recovered, she would always have this holiday in her home.

Thanksgiving morning Dad would take all the kids to visit Uncle Aref and Uncle Sam's family – and sometimes even to visit the Great Uncles, Richard, Ben and Fayadh's homes to wish them all a Happy Thanksgiving.

Our Thanksgiving dinner table was always a feast to behold (and to devour). Apart from the traditional turkey with all the trimmings, mother always served Lebanese food whether it be **Kibbee, Grape Leaves** or other delicious items.

I recall Mom spending every Wednesday, prior to Thanksgiving, baking such delectable pies like **pumpkin, pecan, apple, chocolate cream and lemon meringue**.

Our house was always full of people. Our parents would never let anyone spend a holiday on their own, so we always had last minute guests for Thanksgiving dinner.

After Mother left us, I carried on the Thanksgiving tradition in my home. It has now been passed on to my daughter, Jeannie, who has a house full of company each Thanksgiving Day. She does, however, ask me to keep my fingers in the pie – just as I did with my mother!

Chapter XI

The Diplomatic Years

During the ensuing years, my mother became Mrs. United Nations. Her brother, Uncle Alif had come to New York from Lebanon, with his wife, Aunt Yvette and their children, Mai and Sherine. Uncle Alif was Consul General and later Ambassador to the US and Canada.

Mom spent many a day at the Consulate in New York City, cooking, teaching his staff to prepare and serve, and supervising the meals prepared by his staff for so many of the U.N. delegates and their families.

My Uncle had cocktail and/or dinner parties for 50 - 60 friends, relatives and diplomats and their families at a time and mother was always called upon to supervise The Menu!

The meal on any given day consisted of **Kibbee, Meat Pies, Spinach Pies, Zatar, Cheesebread, Loobie and Rice, Chicken, Hashwi, Hummus, Baba Ghanoush and all kinds of salads.**

It was during the years that Uncle Alif was stationed here as Consul General from Lebanon, that Sito Miriam, Mom's mother, finally came for a visit to America. She was so thrilled to be coming to America and we were so excited to finally meet her.

She asked her grandchildren in Lebanon to teach her to say something wonderful in English when greeting new people in the United States. She practiced her little speech for weeks.

With a houseful of people, my mother proudly introduced her to everyone. With that, Sito Miriam proudly stood up, smiled at the crowd and announced , "Kiss me ass you sonoma bitch."

Everyone roared with laughter and although Mom was slightly shocked and Sito mortified, it quickly became apparent that our cousins had played a cruel joke on her. She was absolutely humiliated and I don't think she ever forgave them. We of course, have always repeated the story and still think it is quite funny.

Since Mom was the best cook in the family, everyone always came to our home for Sunday dinner to enjoy all the Lebanese favorites that filled My mother's Table. On any given day, she would serve **Kibbee, Meat Pies, Hummus, Baba Ghanoush, Chicken, Rice Dressing, Fatoosh, Cheesebread, Syrian Cheese, String Cheese, Kafta and so much more**.

I recall one night, the Patriarch of the Church, was visiting from Lebanon and came to our house for dinner. It was just prior to Christmas when Jeannie woke up ran into the living room, and threw her arms around the Patriarch.

She was just 2 or 3 years old and felt for a certainty it was Santa Claus. The Patriarch was just thrilled with this lovely child, picked her up and hugged her as she kept saying, "I love you, Santa." It was a humorous and enjoyable sight for all.

In those years, Lorraine and I were simply not allowed to help with the cooking. The kitchen was mother's domain and she had full charge of the food. We were, however, always given the privilege of setting the table and washing and drying the dishes.

We were also given the privilege of cleaning the house every Saturday and doing all the ironing! The boys, being sons of course, were exempt from most of these chores!

Chapter XII

School, Love and Marriage

We were all pretty good students. In fact, Lorraine, George and I each skipped a year in high school. I had desperately wanted to be a lawyer but my father did not believe that girls should go to college and so this idea was put aside from my high school days.

As I think back, he most likely felt that way because he had three sons to educate and could not afford to also send two daughters to college. My college education then, came from following the studies of my brothers and cousins who lived with us while completing their education. I edited and typed all reports and term papers.

Lorraine and I both went to work at the age of 17 following our high school graduation. We traveled the subways back and forth to New York City every day. Many an evening tired from the day, we would call my father to pick us up at the train station. I cannot ever recall that he ever refused. How lucky we were to have such a wonderful father.

Lorraine met Dick a few years after she graduated and they were married in May of 1957. For the next two years they lived in Hartford, where Dick was working. In the years that followed they would move back to Brooklyn, then on to Staten Island, and to Alabama and then, they finally settled in New Jersey.

I was just 18 when I met Ed who was 20. It was just one week after he was discharged from the Navy. He was quite different from anyone I had ever known. He was a happy-go-lucky person – a bit on the wild side and my parents felt we were too young to marry. We could not be convinced of this and we were wed in October of 1958. It was sometimes a bumpy road but here we are 45 years later!

When both Lorraine and I left the house, George, Jim and Rick finally had some breathing space in the house.

For the first time in his life, Rick had his own bedroom George and Jimmy shared Lorraine's and my room.

George later moved into Manhattan and, Jimmy and Rick were still living at home when our first child, Edward, Jr., a premature baby, was born, weighing in at 2 lbs. 13 oz., in March of 1964. His weight went down to 2 lbs 8 oz. and we were terrified that he would not survive.

For six weeks we waited patiently each day for the doctors to tell us how he was doing. It was one of the most fearful times in my life. But he was strong and I thank God that we have him today.

Mom and Dad had a two family home and when little Ed was just seven months, we moved into their house "just for a few years." The same month we moved in, I found I was pregnant once again. Those few years ended up lasting over 20 years.

We welcomed Jeannie to our world on July 10, 1965, just 15 months after Eddie was born. She weighed in at 6 lbs. 8 oz. and she proved to be my partner in eating. There was nothing she and I did not like and so began my cooking for two families rather than one. Ed and Little Eddie preferred meat and potatoes while Jean and I preferred **Arabic** food like **Grape Leaves, Looby and Rice, Shash Barak, Koosa and so much more.**

As the family grew, it became incumbent upon me to learn to bake and to make all the Arabic desserts as well as American.

I think I ended up doing a fairly good job of it but could never quite achieve my mother's knack for making certain things. **Caak Ab Haleeb, Caak Shami, Pound Cake, Mahmool, Pumpkin Pie, Apple Pie, Pecan Pie, etc, (secret is the dough) Pineapple Upside Down Cake, Baklava, Mamoul (shortbread)**

My mother and father would have dinner at 5 p.m. and many an evening, without my knowledge, they would ask Jeannie to join them for dinner and then she would come home and have a second dinner with the family!

One evening, Little Ed, who was around four years old, was angry with me and said he was running away from home. I told him I would help him pack his clothes. He put on his baseball hat and packed his baseball glove and a pair of underwear.

We were just sitting for dinner when I bade him farewell and he went out the door. We saw him looking through the window and his father and I were saying how delicious the food was. He finally came back into the house and told us he could not leave because, "I'm not allowed to cross the street."

The boys all got married during the following years. George had moved on to California and he and Marty married and became the proud parents of Christie and Jay.

Jimmy and Gae married and moved to Staten Island and later on settled in New Jersey, and were blessed with Jeffrey, James and Michelle.

Rick and JoAnne left Brooklyn and moved to Austin, Texas with their lovely daughter, Teri in order to be near JoAnne's family.

Our family now was all settled and we truly enjoyed raising our children. This of course, has always been a great joy to us. We loved our children and many of us, wished we had been blessed with more.

Chapter XIII

Learning To Cook

It was during these years that I began to help Mom with the cooking. Well – not exactly the cooking but rather I was the assistant to the cook!   I remember spending many a day rolling **Grape Leaves** to put in the freezer for the winter and many more days chopping cheese for making **Cheesebread** – a favorite of everyone.

In those days, we baked our own dough and chopped all the cheeses. Today we use shredded cheese and store-bought dough when we realized it was almost as good as home made – and far less work.

I have not yet discovered a short way to wrap Grape Leaves. Today, I still spend each Saturday in June picking, cleaning, blanching and rolling grape leaves with **Meat and Rice or Vegetarian style.** I am so happy today that some of my nieces have taken the initiative and now pick and roll their own leaves. In a Lebanese home, there is a grape vine in every yard!

It was, however, during those years I came into my own and my cooking began to improve. I learned to cook most all of the Arabic food but did not really take it seriously until my dear mother passed on in 1981. This task was then passed on to Lorraine and me.

I later diversified into different recipes and also started some of my own after plagiarizing some of the recipes from mother, Lorraine and a variety of friends.

I became a fairly good cook and some of my favorite American/Italian recipes included **Fried Chicken, Stuffed Breast of Chicken, Chicken Parmigianaa, Chicken Casserole, Fried Rice, Meatballs and Spaghetti, Swedish Meatballs, Chicken Soup, String Cheese, Split Pea Soup, Pizza Rustica, Eggplant**

Rollatini, Baked Ziti/Lasagna, Turkey with bread and rice dressing.

Most Sundays were still spent lunching at Mom and Dad's house and she always did the cooking – whether Middle Eastern or American or even Italian in the early days. By then Lorraine and Dick had moved to Alabama and just came for a visit with their children, Lori, Lisa and Linda a few times a year. We were always so happy to see them and could not wait for their visit.

My father retired at 65 and sadly, just six months later, left this world in 1973. It was a terrible shock to the entire family. George and Marty had just married and came to New York for a celebration. We invited 60 people to the house for a wedding party. I had a terrible feeling of foreboding on that day and I remember Dad walking around the house, so proud in his new Glen Plaid suit.

He was a wonderful host. He had previously suffered two heart attacks, and the next morning, he was gone from us forever. It was absolutely dreadful for the entire family. We went from a wedding to a funeral overnight.

We had always felt that mother was the stronger of the two, but my father's passing proved us very wrong. She was very strong, but this was the most difficult time of her life for mother and indeed for all of us, but we had to learn to live with the loss of a loved one and we shall always have nothing but good memories of this kind and generous man.

Chapter XIV

A New Career

The following year, I returned to work in a temp agency and the children were left in the care of my mother. She began cooking for my family and we enjoyed her delicious dinners each evening.

When I went to work, allegedly for one week at Dow Jones, I met Victor Webb. He convinced me to stay at Dow Jones and to work full time as his assistant. He had just transferred to the US from London as the International Director of Dow Jones publications. It was a new and wonderful experience for me.

I met so many people from around the world and one of our duties was to wine and dine visitors from far away places like Hong Kong, Australia, Japan, Singapore, London, to name a few, in the very best restaurants in New York.

Among my phobias were fear of heights and fear of flying. I recall the first time I went to the top of the World Trade Center for dinner at Windows on the World. I was absolutely terrified going up the elevator to the 102nd floor, but once there, fell in love with the restaurant and the sights of the city and ultimately spent many evenings taking clients and visitors for drinks or dinner. I always had a wonderful time.

A whole new world opened up for me and I went from Madlene Olson, housewife, to Madlene Olson, Executive Assistant. I truly enjoyed my most interesting job.

As the years progressed, I became an International Media Specialist and visited many cities throughout the United States and beyond – London, Paris and the entire Caribbean.

My fear of flying vanished to a degree as did my fear of heights. I still do not like flying, but have come to know and accept that it is the only way to see the world.

It has been a fabulous experience and I am so thankful for the wonderful opportunity given to me. I learned so much from Victor and I am so happy that my experience gave my children the opportunity to visit so many of the places I had been when we went on vacations.

Working full time, my cooking was obviously not as exotic as it was when I was at home. It became too much for mother for prepare dinner for us at such a late hour. She and my father always sat for dinner at 5 p.m. and I was not home before 7. And so dinners became quick-cooking items – although none of us has ever looked as though we were hungry.

After seven years at Dow Jones, in March of 1981 Victor and I left the Wall Street Journal to open our own business in the international marketing, public relations and advertising field.

Two weeks after we opened the business, mother was hospitalized and forever left us on Good Friday, April 17, at the age of 68. It was not until after Mom was gone that Lorraine and I really began preparing the Arabic foods.

Chapter XV
My Sister and Me

Lorraine, Dick and their family had by then moved back to New Jersey. Each of us would alter Mom's recipes somewhat and then we would argue over the exact ingredients or measurements that went into her original recipe.

Today, as I think back, it could well be that my mother did not really remember how much of what goes into what. And I can now vouch for that simply because I have become my mother!

Once again, it is important to remember - cooking is an art and testing and tasting is the only true way to really measure ingredients - salt, pepper, and other spices. But for most Middle East beginners, it is hit or miss initially and then finally most of the food tastes pretty good. And no one knows or really cares whether it's a teaspoon of baking power or baking soda!

It was during the years after mother was gone that "The Menu" really entered our lives. Lorraine and I took over cooking for all the holidays and Thanksgiving was spent at my house and Christmas at hers. For the most part, we both ended up making Turkey with all the Lebanese style trimmings.

We almost always included some kind of **Pasta and Grape Leaves. A typical meal consisted of Turkey, Spiral Sliced Ham, Rice Stuffing (Hashwi), Bread Stuffing, Mashed Potatoes, Sweet Potatoes, Mashed Turnips, Broccoli Casserole, Grape Leaves, Pasta, Hummus, Baba Ghanoush, Cheesebread, Spinach Dip, Artichoke Dip, Salad and of course, Cranberry Sauce**

Jimmy and his wife, Gae and their children, Jeffrey, James and Michelle had moved to New Jersey about an hour away from us. George, Marty and Christie and Jay were in California and Ricky, JoAnne and Teri were in Texas. Each year one of the families would come to visit and Lorraine and I would agonize for weeks over "The Menu."

We knew the boys enjoyed Arabic food but we also wanted a variety of American and Italian food, so we would each choose different meals to prepare. **Mjadarah (Lentils and Rice), Arabic Cole Slaw, Looby and Rice, Tabooli, and all the staples such as Kibbee and Meat Pies.**

For those who wanted alternatives to Lebanese food, we always included an American or Italian dish of some kind. The favorites were **Chicken or Veal parmigiana, Lasagna, Baked Penne, Baked Ziti, and, of course, Hamburgers and Hot Dogs with Dad's famous Chili.**

For an absolute certainty, we both always had to make **Caak Ab Haleeb** (Easter Cakes). Most of the family preferred that to food! So we always had a huge supply when they came to visit.

Chapter XVI

A Weekend Retreat

In 1993, Ed and I decided to buy a summer house on Lindy's Lake in New Jersey. We were still living in Brooklyn at the time and wanted someplace to go for weekends and holidays. We came to love that house and found many new friends.

We always had a barbecue at our house or at a friend's and apart from **Spareribs, Hamburgers, Hot Dogs, Steaks, and London Broil,** we also made **Chili, Cold and Hot Potato Salad, Seven Layer Salad and Baked Ziti.**

In country living, each family brings something to these barbeques. I was usually called upon to make **Fried Chicken and a Pasta Dish.** Middle Eastern food was not as popular as it is today so I primarily cooked American or Italian food – except of course when the family came to the lake.

Everyone enjoyed the house. We all had such a wonderful time swimming in the lake and our dogs were in absolute heaven. They would simply jump off the deck and swim around the lake to their hearts content.

Most of our summer vacations and weekends were spent at the lake for ten years. There was always a house full of company and we had a great time. My partner, Victor Webb and his wife, Wendy, enjoyed West Milford so much that they sold their house in Short Hills and bought a home on four acres of land in West Milford. Today, they have created a beautiful English garden on the land with three ponds.

Unfortunately, my husband, Ed, became incapacitated in 1999. There was no apparent reason but he was simply unable to walk. We are, of course, praying for a miracle, but

I fear he is destined to spend the rest of his days in a wheel-chair.

After a year and many hospital and rehabilitation visits, he was ultimately diagnosed with diabetic neuropathy and much to our sadness, we had to sell our lovely weekend home. It simply became impossible for me to care for the two houses.

Chapter XVII

Our Share of Sadness

A year before we bought the Summer house, much to our extreme shock and total sadness, my brother Jimmy, at the young age of 47, had a massive heart attack while he was sleeping and was forever gone from us.

It was a horrendous shock and loss to the entire family, and we knew then, that life would never be the same. For the rest of our lives, there has and always will be a void in our heart that can never be filled.

Although I had not see him as often as I would have liked, Jimmy and I spoke to each fairly often on the telephone – either one calling the other when we had a moment. I have always regretted not calling him just prior to his death. I shall miss him forever.

And when it rains, it pours. In August of 2001, I was, quite by accident, while having a test on my blood, diagnosed with cardiac problems and was told that I needed to have quintuple bypass surgery. It came of course, as a big surprise and as a rude awakening and somewhat of a shock since I had believed I had taken care of myself and was fairly healthy. For some unknown reason, I had no fear going into surgery.

I spent 17 days in the hospital and almost anything that could go wrong, did go wrong. I was totally out of touch with the world the first week. I needed blood transfusions, my lungs had to be aspirated and my pressure zoomed. Jeannie, Eddie and Lorraine spent many long hours at the hospital worrying about me and waiting for me to wake up. Finally, Jeannie insisted they take me off all pain medication and after that, I woke and started the long road back to feeling human again.

I finally came home the first week in September to recuperate. It was not easy initially and shortly after I arrived home, while watching the news on television with Victor, who had brought me the office mail that morning, New York City was hit by the 9/11 disaster.

Initially, we thought it was an accident but as we were watching the television, the second plane hit the second tower as we stood there in shock. It was inconceivable to us and to the rest of the world that this could happen. But it did and the event had had a terrible affect on the whole world.

Working for me was put on hold for the next few months. Once I began to feel better, Victor brought work home to me and I started working and doing light cooking once again. It seemed like an eternity that I was at home, but the time passed and everything I felt had gone back to normal.

But this was not to be. History, unfortunately, repeats itself, and our darling Lorraine at the age of 68, left this world just six months later and left all of us in a complete state of despair, unexpectedly in June of 2002. Her loss was almost more than we could bear. I thank God each day for giving us the support of each other that we all needed at this terrible time.

Lorraine was not only my sister, but she was my best friend - even my soul mate. We were about as close as two sisters could possibly be. Like any other sisters, we had our disagreements – but we never left each other angry or not speaking.

She had triple bypass surgery just nine months after my surgery. I was very frightened for her but felt certain she would be fine after my ordeal. She came through her surgery like the trooper she was.

She felt great after the first day and was due to go home just five days after the surgery. Tragically, she suddenly developed a blood clot and was gone on the morning she was coming home. I recall talking to her on the phone the night before – it was the only night I did not visit her – and I told her I loved her and she said the same to me. I know I shall spend the rest of my life mourning and missing her.

I recall telling so many people who came to her funeral that she was my best friend – and the response from so many of these people was, "She was also my best friend." What a legacy to leave! Over 600 people attended her funeral. She was so very special to everyone who knew her!

Chapter XVIII
My Family and Me

It seems we pass so quickly from spring to autumn and sometimes, as I sit and ponder my life, I think how have the "Golden Years" come so quickly? And where have all the other years gone so quickly?

Life will never be the same without Lorraine and Jimmy. We think of them each day but we do know that life goes on and we have all tried our best to adjust.

After Lorraine left us, my children and some of my nieces began asking for different recipes, most of which we had never really written down. Most of them were in our heads.

One day, a few of my nieces called and came to my house for a cooking lesson. We prepared **Grape Leaves, Meat Pies, Spinach Pies and Syrian Cheese**.

It was a few months later that I conceived the idea that I should to put pen to paper – or should I say, fingers to computer - and write down the recipes that I have prepared over the years. And so I began typing away.

As I continued to write, the story expanded, and it occurred to me that many in our family were not aware of our history. Therefore I felt, with the help of my brother George, I would combine the two. We are and always have been a very close-knit family and we have a heritage of which we can be proud.

And so, as you begin to formulate your own recipes and prepare the delicious foods of our Lebanese people, I hope my recipes will serve you all well.

Bon Appetit!

The Menu

These are some of my favorites. In fact, they are most of my recipes. I love cooking and I also love eating! Cooking is so much easier today than in the time of my mother. In most cases, I take all short cuts and I am still told that my food is quite good. Now most of my secrets come out!

I use dried onions and garlic for nearly all recipes. When I specifically say to use a clove of garlic, use fresh garlic. Dried does not work well with some recipes. Let the salt and pepper be your decision. It is not included in many recipes but most people enjoy the seasoning so be an entrepreneur and do your own thing!

For **Cheesebread, Zatar, Meat Pies and Spinach Pies**, I now use store-bought Bridgeford Dough rather than making my own but have included my home made dough recipe here.

I have learned over the years, that most times shortcuts taste just as good as the long way around. Well, perhaps not - but let's just say that I have not had any complaints.

And so, I leave all of this to you, the cooks of today and the cooks of tomorrow. You will, as I have done through the years, in all likelihood change many of my recipes in some way to suit your own taste and that of your family. But don't be afraid – you stand every chance of your foods tasting much better than mine.

Once again, **Bon Appetit!**

The Menu

NOTES

Breakfast

Breakfast

TIP: Everything obviously tastes best with butter – but if you are watching your waistline and/or for health reasons – choose olive oil for most of your cooking.

Corned Beef Hash

Left over potatoes and corned beef or sliced from the market may be used for this recipe.

½ lb corned beef, cubed	2 potatoes, cubed
1/8 stick butter	1 egg white
onion flakes	salt and pepper

Saute beef, potatoes and onions in butter. Whip egg white with a fork and slowly drizzle over the mixture. Serve immediately.

For variations, add two raw eggs to the mixture and fry on a high flame until browned. You can also fry eggs on the side and top the beef.

Breakfast Quiche

This was my sister, Lorraine's, recipe and it is absolutely delicious!

10 eggs	1 lb cottage cheese
½ cup flour	1 lb. grated Monterey Jack Cheese
½ tsp salt	1 tsp baking powder
1 stick butter	

Melt butter, beat eggs, mix all ingredients. Bake at 400 degrees for 15 minutes. Lower to 350 and bake additional 35-40 minutes.

French Toast

This is a quick and simple recipe that is enjoyed by every-one.

1 egg	6 slices of any kind of bread
¼ cup milk	1 tsp cinnamon
pinch salt	2 tbsp sugar

Thoroughly mix all ingredients except the bread. Heat butter over medium flame and dip slices of bread into the mixture. Fry for just one minute on each side. Serve with butter and syrup.

Pancakes

This recipe is so simple and always works!

1 cup flour	2 tbsp oil or melted butter
1 egg	½ cup sugar
1 tsp baking powder	1 cup milk
1 tsp vanilla	

To this, you may add blueberries or strawberries but this is optional.

Mix all ingredients thoroughly and pour ¾ cup on to hot greased fry pan. When bubbles come up, turn over for 30 seconds. Butter and syrup to taste.

Swedish Pancakes

Same recipe as Pancakes but omit the baking powder and mix with fork so the batter is lumpy. Grease pan and pour ½ cup batter into pan and swirl around. When batter is dry, flip over for 10 seconds. Put fork into side and curl up like a crepe. Immediately butter the pancake and roll up once again. I do not advise using fresh fruit in these pancakes.

This is a great recipe that can be used with syrup or filled with sweetened ricotta or cottage cheese and any kind of fruit. Make your own!!

NOTES

Appetizers

TIP: Salt, pepper and any other condiments are used according to taste. A good cook simply must taste their food while preparing. This surely accounts for most good cooks having a weight problem! It is not included in many recipes but most people enjoy experimenting with the seasonings so be an entrepreneur and do your own thing!

Antipasto Tray

This is not a recipe but rather a platter. I have been asked to prepare this for many family events we have had through the years. It is a hit at any party. Serve alone or with other appetizers.

½ pkg baby carrots	6 stalks celery cut up
3 cucumbers cut in rounds	3 pcs red roasted peppers
½ lb. provolone cut in cubes	broccoli crowns
½ lb. Genoa salami	½ lb. sliced pepperoni
3 pcs fresh mozzarella, sliced	6 devilled eggs
6 green olives with pimento	6 black olives

Layer the carrots, celery, cucumbers and broccoli crowns around the outside of the platter. Put eggs in the center. Roll the salami and put over the veggies. Add the mozzarella and put a small piece of roasted pepper over each piece. Add the cubed provolone and olives. It should be a sight to behold. You can add any other items you wish like radishes, pickles, etc.

Hummus

This is the staple appetizer in any Lebanese home. It has become a favorite of all nationalities.

1 can chick peas	1 large clove garlic	parsley
2 tbsp tahini	2 tbsp olive oil	salt

Empty half the water from chick peas and put into food processor together with all other ingredients, until creamy. Garnish with parsley and drizzle olive oil.

Baba Ghanoush

This is the companion appetizer to Hummus.

1 eggplant	1 clove garlic	1 tsp salt
2 tbsp tahini	2 tbsp yogurt	1 tbsp olive oil

Bake whole eggplant in microwave or on grill until soft. Remove pulp and put into food processor with all other ingredients. Garnish with parsley.

Broccoli Casserole

Another recipe where you can change the cheese, add mushrooms, or whatever you choose. It is delicious not matter how it is made.

1 head broccoli	½ lb. Velveeta or sharp cheddar cheese
onion flakes	½ cup grated cheese
¾ cup milk	salt and pepper
croutons	

Cook broccoli, cut into bite-size pieces and arrange in 9 x 12 baking pan. Melt cheese with milk with all ingredients. Pour mixture over the broccoli and then sprinkle with croutons. Bake at 350 for 30 minutes.

Cheesebread

This was one of my mother's specialties. Almost any cheeses can be used, but the basic recipe always includes Velveeta and sharp cheddar.

1 pkg Bridgeford dough	½ cup oil
2 pkg. sharp cheddar	1 pkg. mild cheddar
1 pkg mozzarella	3 tsp baking powder
1 pkg crumbled bleu cheese	¼ cup black fennel seeds
1 pkg. crumbled feta cheese	1 cup olive oil
1 onion or 1 tbsp dried onion	1 small box Velveeta
¾ cup flour	¼ cup anise seeds

Defrost dough until it is soft and pliable. Each loaf makes 4 loaves of cheesebread. Spread each piece of dough on baking sheet after dipping in Mazola Oil. Mix all other ingredients.

Take a portion of the cheese (about a large handful and pat in hands until flat. Then pat onto dough. Let stand for about 5 minutes before putting into oven at 375 degrees for approximately 15 –20 minutes. If the cheese is dry, pat with a little olive or canola oil.

This is actually a lot easier to make than it sounds, especially with the advent of store-bought dough, dried onions, and shredded cheeses! You can however, use my home made dough recipe!

TIP: To make life easier, use dried onions and garlic for nearly all recipes unless it specifically says to use a clove of garlic, use fresh garlic. Dried does not work well with some recipes. Let the salt and pepper be your decision.

Deviled Eggs

Great appetizer!

6 eggs	2 tbsp mayonnaise
1 tbsp Mustard	2 tbsp relish

Boil eggs in salt water for 7 minutes after coming to a boil. Peel, cut in half and

Remove and mash yolks. Mix yokes with other ingredients and fill egg halves with mixture. Garnish with small piece of parsley, olive, or pickle.

TIP: Boiling eggs in salt water makes it easier to peel.

Fish with Tahini

This recipe can be made with most any kind of flaked fish. I use tuna because I like it and it's easy.

1 can tuna fish drained	3 tbsp tahini paste
lemon juice	1 clove mashed garlic
¼ cup chopped parsley	1/8 cup pignolia nuts
approx ½ cup water	1/8 cup butter

Mix tahini with water until it becomes creamy and can be poured. Add lemon juice, garlic, and parsley. Saute pignolia nuts in butter. Flake tuna fish and put on plate. Pour tahini mixture over tuna and then add buttered nuts.

Garnish with sprigs of parsley or black olives. Serve with pita bread or crackers.

Kibbee (raw)

Mother was the best at making this. It's one of those recipe's my sister, Lorraine and I always argued over the ingredients but no matter which of us made it, it always tasted good.

2 lbs. extra lean ground lamb	2 tbsp marjoram
2 cups fine bulgar	¾ cup finely minced onion
2 tbsp allspice	salt and pepper
¼ cup olive oil	

Mix all ingredients and knead for several minutes adding a bit of ice water.   Garnish with parsley and/or raw onion. Drizzle olive oil over meat and serve.

See Middle East entrees for cooked Kibbee.

Meatless Grape Leaves

This is a delicious appetizer which is normally served at room temperature.

100 Leaves (See Grape Leaves under Middle East entrees for blanching.)

¾ cup rice	4 tomatoes cubed
1 small onion	¼ cup minced mint
¼ cup minced parsley	1 small can chick peas
1/2 cup lemon juice	allspice

Mix all ingredients. Lay leaves flat and add small amount of mixture. Turn in sides and roll. Cook on medium heat with 2 cups water, 2 tbsp salt and ½ cup lemon juice and a sliced tomato for approximately 40 minutes until rice is fluffy.

TIP: Many times I split the package of dough and make half cheesebread and half meat pies and/or spinach pies at the same time.

Spinach Pies

I have never been able to master making perfect triangles like my Mother. Good luck to anyone who can. The saving grace is the taste!

<table>
<tr><td>1 Pkg Bridgeford Dough</td><td>6 boxes spinach</td></tr>
<tr><td>salt and pepper</td><td>dry or fresh onions</td></tr>
<tr><td>½ cup olive oil</td><td>flour</td></tr>
<tr><td>½ cup lemon juice</td><td></td></tr>
</table>

Cook spinach with onions, olive oil, lemon, and salt and pepper. Defrost dough until soft and pliable (overnight in refrigerator or on the counter for 1-2 hours) Pat golf ball size pieces of dough on cookie sheet with flour.

Drain spinach mixture (put juice aside) and put a full tablespoon of the mixture in the dough. Pinch sides to form triangle. Reinforce triangle with flour. It's a little tricky to form the triangles but practice makes perfect!

Bake at 350 for approximately 15 minutes, Remove from oven and dip into left over spinach juice

TIP: Crushed red pepper is a wonderful substitute for black pepper in Italian food.

Eggplant Rollatini

This is great when cooking an Italian dinner and can be used either as an appetizer or a side dish. I can even eat it as a meal!

<table>
<tr><td>1 eggplant sliced thin</td><td>flour/salt and pepper</td></tr>
<tr><td>1 cup ricotta</td><td>1 cup shredded mozzarella</td></tr>
<tr><td>1 egg</td><td>grated cheese</td></tr>
</table>

1 can tomato paste seasoned with oregano/minced onion/ minced garlic/salt and pepper/olive oil/basil/ parsley.

Mix tomato paste with water and all other ingredients and cook over medium flame for one half hour. Salt and Pepper eggplant and put between paper towels to drain for one half hour. Dip eggplant in flour/salt and pepper and fry in Canola or olive oil.

Mix ricotta/mozzarella/egg together and spoon full tablespoon into each piece of fried eggplant roll. Place face down in baking pan. Cover with tomato sauce and sprinkle with grated cheese. Cook 20 minutes at 350.

This is a great side dish to spaghetti and meatballs or even plain penne with sauce for vegetarians.

Eggplant Parmigiana

This is another great side dish when cooking an Italian dinner, but can be used as

1 eggplant sliced thin	salt and pepper
1 cup ricotta	1 cup shredded mozzarella
1 egg	grated cheese
1 can tomato paste	½ cup breadcrumb/flour mixture

1 can tomato sauce seasoned with oregano/minced onion/ minced garlic/salt and pepper/olive oil/basil/ parsley.

Mix tomato paste sauce with water and all other ingredients and cook over medium flame for one half hour.

Salt and pepper eggplant and lay between paper towels to drain for one half hour. Dip eggplant in flour/salt and pepper and fry in Canola or Olive oil.

 Mix ricotta, mozzarella, egg and grated cheese. Layer tomato sauce, followed by eggplant and ricotta mixture. Repeat layers. Cover top with mozzarella and grated cheese and bake for one hour. Let sit for 20 minutes before serving.

TIP: Baking time of nearly all recipes really depends on the oven – so practice to find the right temperature.

Sausage Rolls

This recipe came from the British! My business partner, first introduced us to sausage rolls and they are liked by most everyone. Some people like them a little spicier and add onions, soy sauce, Worcestershire sauce or whatever they want to original mixture.

 1 pkg Pepperidge Farm Flaky Pastry
 3/4 cup breadcrumbs   1 pkg breakfast sausage loose

Mix sausage and breadcrumbs. Roll out pastry dough and place sausage flat. Roll dough and cut into 1" strips. Use fork to make holes on top of each sausage roll. Bake for approximately 35minutes at 300 degrees. These are yummy English appetizers usually enjoyed by all.

Shrimp Cocktail

This is a wonderful starter for a formal dinner. Not bad as a pass around plate either.

 1 lb. shrimp   salt
 1 cup lemon juice   water

Fill saucepan with shrimp, salt and water. Let come to a boil for one minute and remove from heat and pour cold water over shrimp. For crisp shrimp soak overnight in water, lemon juice and salt. Rinse thoroughly next day and serve with cocktail sauce made with ketchup, horseradish, and Worcestershire Sauce.

Zatar

I love this for either breakfast or lunch with Lebanee (see misc.) or with sliced tomatoes.

1 pkg Bridgeford Dough	½ cup sumac
½ cup zatar	1 cup olive or canola oil

Defrost dough until pliable. Cut each loaf into 4 pieces and spread on baking sheet after lightly dipping in oil.

Mix sumac and zatar and add oil. (I usually buy the combined ingredients and refrigerate them for use later. It will last over a year refrigerated)

Spread 1 ½ tablespoons of the mixture and pat on to each piece of dough. Let sit for 5 minutes and bake in oven at 375" for approximately 10 minutes.

Soup

Soup

TIP: On a cold winter night, add less water to the soup and it becomes a stew!

Chicken with Rice or Noodles

This is my basic recipe. Other vegetables may be added such as mushrooms, peas, to make the soup like a stew that can be used as an entrée on a cold winter night.

3 chicken breasts	4 packets chicken bouillon
1 tsp parsley	2 tbsp lemon juice
1 pkg baby carrots cut in half	salt and pepper
1 pkg. noodles or 1 cup rice	6 stalks celery chopped
1 tsp dried onions	1 cinnamon stick

Boil chicken with celery and carrots and all other ingredients except rice/noodles. When chicken is cooked, remove from water and cut or shred into bite size pieces and return to pot. When celery is soft, add rice or noodles until cooked (rice 20 minutes, noodles 15 minutes).

Chicken may be boneless, skinless or on the bones – my quick easy way is boneless.

Creamed Chicken

The same as above, but prior to adding the cut/shredded chicken, dissolve ¼ cup flour in water. Add 1/8 lb. butter and one cup milk and then add half amount of rice/noodles. Delicious but obviously more calories!!

Lentil Soup

This is a great soup for the vegetarians. Just leave off the bouillon if you like.

½ pkg lentils	2 cups sliced or diced carrots
1 cup diced celery	1 sliced onion
1 bay leaf	salt and pepper
2 beef/chicken boullion cubes	

Mix all ingredients in 4-6 cups water. Bring to boil and simmer for two hours or until lentils are soft.

Split Pea

My all time favorite soup. Many add potatoes to make it an entrée.

1 pkg split peas	1 ham steak or ham bone
1 bay leaf	½ pkg carrots cut in 1" pieces
6 stalks cubed celery	salt and pepper
1 tbsp onion flakes	

Rinse peas and fill pot with water. Add all ingredients together and cook for 2-3 hours on medium flame. If soup becomes too thick add water and reheat.

One of my favorites – some people add potatoes – starchy but good!

Vegetable Soup

You can use your imagination for this. Add any vegetable you like.

3 packets chicken/beef boullion	2 quarts water
2 cut up fresh tomatoes	1 cup peas
1 cup chopped celery	1 chopped onion
1 cup chopped carrots	1 chopped potato
1 can kidney beans	1 can white beans
salt and pepper	1 bay leaf
1 tsp dried parsley	

Just mix all ingredients and cook covered on medium heat until all vegetables are cooked.

NOTES

Salads

Salads

TIP: I use dried onions and garlic (with a few exceptions) but you can use fresh any time.

Asparagus Salad

This is a great and easy summer salad that can be prepared in advance.

6 asparagus spears	2 tomatoes
1 jar mushrooms	3 tbsp Wishbone Balsamic Vinegar

Lightly steam asparagus. Cut in 1" sections. Slice tomatoes. Mix all ingredients and serve or refrigerate.   To this you can add oregano, parsley, basil, zatar and you can also use any balsamic vinegar and olive oil.

Chicken Salad

I use boneless white meat chicken, but with leftovers, you can use any kind and this recipe is also good for turkey salad.

3 boneless chicken breasts	1 cup cubed celery
2 tbsps white vinegar	2 tbsps
2 tbsps canola oil	3 tbsos mayonnaise

Boil breasts, let cool and cube into bite-size pieces. Mix all ingredients; garnish with parsley, egg halves, tomatoes or olives, etc.

Seven Layer Salad

This is a great summer recipe which we have made for many barbeques.

½ head lettuce chopped	½ lb. shredded cheddar
6 strips crumbled bacon	½ pkg peas
3 cubed tomatoes	6 sliced eggs
any dressing you like	1 cup croutons

Layer each item in deep bowl – ie ¼ lettuce; ¼ cheddar, eggs, tomatoes, etc. except croutons, and make second layer. When ready to serve, drizzle dressing over the top of the salad and serve immediately.

Tabooli

Except for my husband, Ed, I have yet to find someone who does not like Tabooli. Now that I have said it, those who don't will probably come out of the woodwork.

2 bunches parsley	1 cup bulgar
3 tomatoes	½ cup lemon juice
1 tbsp dried onions	½ cup olive oil
salt and pepper	½ cup mint

Wash parsley and mint several times – finely chop in food processor. Chop tomatoes, mix all ingredients and refrigerate. Can be served immediately but usually tastes best after a few hours. It can remain in the refrigerator for three days.

Tip: You can repace ¼ cup fresh mint with one tablespoon dried mint.

Shepherd Salad

This was one of our family's favorite salads. It originated in a Turkish restaurant.

3 large tomatoes	1 tbsp dried onions
2 Cucumbers	¼ cup Balsamic vinegar
1 tbsp Sugar	½ cup olive oil
¼ cup white vinegar	2 tbsps chopped parsley
salt and pepper	

Cube tomatoes and cucumbers. Mix and add all other ingredients and serve. Can be refrigerated up to one week.

TIP: For many of my salads, I use Wishbone Balsamic Vinegar Dressing – but any balsamic or white vinegar will do. Just dress it up with spices, lemon and olive oil.

Middle East Cole Slaw

This was my favorite cole slaw. It compliments Mjardarrah (lentils and rice) No kissing after eating!

1 pkg or ½ shredded cabbage   1 clove mashed garlic
½ cup Lemon   ½ cup white vinegar
½ cup olive oil   salt and pepper to taste

Mix all ingredients and serve or refrigerate up to 2 weeks.

American Cole Slaw

This is the basic recipe that you can alter according to taste.

1 pkg or ½ shredded cabbage   1 cup mayonnaise
¼ cup lemon   1 tbsp minced onions
½ cup milk   salt and pepper
½ cup shredded carrots

Mix all ingredients and serve or refrigerate up to 3days.

Mixed Salad - Middle Eastern

This salad is the staple salad served on a Middle Eastern dinner table. They would never think of using a bottled dressing.

½ pkg or ½ head lettuce 1 cucumber – sliced in rounds
2 tomatoes   1 head mashed garlic
salt and pepper   oregano to taste
½ cup lemon juice   ½ cup white vinegar
½ cup olive oil

Mix all ingredients and serve immediately.

Fatoosh

This salad is so delicious it can be eaten as a meal – particularly if you are a vegetarian.

2 loaves pita bread toasted	2 tomatoes
2 cups sliced or chopped lettuce	onion flakes
1 cucumber in rounds	olive oil
1/8 cup zatar	1/8 cup lemon

Break toasted pita bread into bite size pieces. Mix all ingredients and serve immediately. Can be refrigerated but the bread will become soggy – still tastes good!

My Mixed Salad

I always take the short cut – but this sure is good.

½ pkg or ½ head lettuce	1 cucumber – sliced in rounds
2 tomatoes	salt and pepper
1 cup croutons	¼ cup zatar
½ cup Wishbone Balsamic Vinegar	
½ cup shredded grated cheese	

Mix all ingredients and serve immediately. You can also add onions, Baco Bits, sunflower seeds and the kitchen sink if you want!

My Tomato and Onion Salad

This is a favorite summer time salad. It is particularly good with home grown tomatoes.

4 medium tomatoes	1 small onion
1 tbsp zatar	½ tsp oregano crushed
½ tsp crushed basil	balsamic vinegar
2 tbsp lemon juice	olive oil

Slice tomatoes away from core into bite size pieces. Slice onion in rounds. Mix with rest of ingredients. This is hit or miss, you will find your own taste with salt, etc. An easy way to make this delicious salad is to use Wishbone Balsamic Vinegar dressing. Just add the other spices.

Cucumbers and Yogurt

This is a great, refreshing summer salad which is best served with a rice dish such as chicken and rice or grape leaves.

2 cups yogurt	1 clove mashed garlic
1 sliced cucumber	1 tbsp dried mint
salt and pepper to taste	

Mix all ingredients and serve. Can be refrigerated for a week.

Potatoes

Potatoes

TIP: For most recipes that call for boiled potatoes, do not use Idaho. They tend to fall apart when boiling.

Breakfast Home Fried Potatoes

Like chicken, there are so many ways to cook a potato

6 potatoes	1/8 lb butter
¼ cup oil	salt and pepper

Heat oil and butter on medium flame. Add potatoes and cook covered for approximately 12-15 minutes. Uncover and stir occasionally. When potatoes are cooked, flame can be increased to brown to your liking.

Lunch/Dinner Home Fried Potatoes

These potatoes deliciously compliment meat or fowl.

6 potatoes	1/8 lb butter
¼ cup oil	salt and pepper
½ cup grated cheese	1 small onion or flakes

Heat oil and butter and add potatoes, onion, salt and pepper. Cover and stir occasionally. When browning, add grated cheese and serve immediately.

Potato Salad

This is an easy recipe that should be prepared prior to serving.

5 lbs potatoes boiled	1 cup chopped celery
½ cup lemon	6 chopped hard boiled eggs
½ cup vinegar	1 minced onion or flakes
½ cup oil	½ cup mayonnaise
¼ cup milk	salt and pepper

Cut potatoes into bite size pieces and while warm add all ingredients except milk and mayonnaise. For best results refrigerate this overnight and then add other ingredients. Garnish with half the boiled eggs, parsley and tomatoes.

Potato Salad – Middle East

This recipe is the same as American potato salad, except add ½ cup chopped parsley and omit the mayonnaise and milk.

Whipped Potatoes

Can anyone resist whipped potatoes?

    5 lbs. boiled potatoes   ¼ lb butter
    1 cup milk   salt and pepper

Whip potatoes with hand or electric mixer until creamy. Add all other ingredients and serve or place under broiler for a delicious crust.

Potatoes and Eggs

When home fried potatoes are cooked, add scrambled eggs and stir until eggs are cooked.

Twice Baked Potatoes

This is the basic recipe which most everyone likes. Any cheese you like can be used.

    2 baked potatoes   ½ cup shredded cheese
    ¼ cup milk   salt and pepper
    1 tbsp butter

Cut potatoes in half. Remove from skin and mash with milk, cheese, butter and salt and pepper. Bake in oven for 20 minutes. Variations include bacon topping or bacon mixed with ingredients.

Warm Potato Salad

Not a very slenderizing salad, but who can resist the delicious taste.

5 lbs potatoes boiled	1minced onion or flakes
1 cup chopped celery	6 chopped hard boiled eggs
¾ cup mayonnaise	8 strips crumbled bacon
salt and pepper	½ lb. cheddar cheese
¼ cup milk.	

Mix all ingredients except half the bacon and cheese. Mixture should be creamy. You may have to add a little more mayonnaise. Place in 9 x 12 pan and sprinkle the balance of the bacon and cheddar cheese over the top. Bake at 350 for about ½ hour until slightly browned. Serve immediately

Sweet Potatoes - Candied

There are so many ways to candy sweet potatoes. I like this recipe

4 sweet potatoes	2 cups brown sugar
1 tsp cinnamon	1 tsp pumpkin pie spice
1/8 stick butter	1 tsp allspice
1 tsp nutmeg	

Melt brown sugar together with spices in 2 cups of water. Peel potatoes and cut in quarters or halves, depending on size of potatoes. Lay potatoes in 9 x 12 pan and pour sugar mixture over it. Apply a dab of butter on each piece. Bake at 375 for approximately 40 minutes or until potatoes are soft.

Whipped Sweet Potatoes

These are wonderful and can be topped with marshmallows and broiled for a few minutes prior to serving.

4 sweet potatoes	½ stick butter
1 cup maple syrup	1 cubed carrot
½ tsp nutmeg	½ tsp allspice

Cook potatoes and carrot until soft. Whip and add butter and syrup.

Entrees Middle Eastern

TIP: Most Middle Eastern food is historically made with Lamb. Even those who do not care for leg of lamb or lamb chops are happy with the flavor of lamb in our foods.

Kibbee (Cooked)

This is the staple entrée in most all Middle East homes, particularly when having company.

Same ingredients as raw Kibbee (see appetizers)

Additional Ingredients –Filling:

¼ cup pignolia nuts	¼ cup minced/chopped onions
½ lb. ground lamb	½ lb. butter
¼ cup olive oil	allspice
¾ cup plain yogurt	salt and pepper

Saute pignolia nuts in butter in ¼ lb. butter until brown. Add ground lamb and onions and mix well. Cool down and add yogurt and mix.

Line bottom of 9 x 12 pan with part of butter. Pat into pancake shapes in hand and apply to bottom of pan until covered across, approx ½ - ¾." Add filling and cover top with balance of meat. Wet hands in water and lightly pat full pan. Cut pieces in the tray into diamond and/or cubes. Pour butter over top of meat and drizzle oil over entire tray.

Bake at 375 degrees for approximately an hour to one and one half hours.

Home Made Dough

For those who like to cook from scratch – like I did years ago – I have included the home made dough recipe that can be used for meat pies, spinach pies, cheesebread and zatar – or just plain pita bread.

6 cups flour   ¼ cup oil
½ cup Crisco   3 packets yeast
2 cups of milk

Mix all ingredients about two hours before using. Let the dough rise (covered) to approximately double its size (2 hours) – and it is ready to use.

Meat Pies

This is another "must serve" for Lebanese company dinners.

1 pkg Bridgeford Dough   ¾ cup pignolia nuts
1 stick butter   2 lbs ground lamb
3 tbsp onions   2 tbsp allspice
1 cup plain yogurt   salt and pepper

Saute pignolia nuts in butter until brown. Add lamb and onions and salt and pepper and sauté until pink is gone. Remove from heat and add yogurt.

Cut dough in size of golf balls. Use flour to flatten dough on baking sheets. Add full tablespoon of meat filling and spread out on baking sheets. Bake at 375 approximately 15 minutes.

Grape Leaves

Grape Leaves can be purchased in any Middle East or Greek Store in a jar, but most Middle East families have their own vine. The most tender leaves are pickedin late May and during the month of June. They are normally blanched, filled and frozen for use throughout the winter.

100 leaves   1 lb ground lamb (or beef)
1 cup white rice   1 full tsp allspice
½ cup water   salt and pepper
cinnamon stick   breast of lamb bone or piece of chicken
¼ cup soft butter ½ cup lemon (to taste)

Boil the lamb bone with salt and pepper/cinnamon stick for approximately ½ hour or until a little tender and put aside.

Boil a pot of water with salt. Wash leaves carefully. When water comes to a boil, turn flame off and put leaves into the boiling water for 5 minutes. Remove and rinse thoroughly with cold water. These leaves are now blanched and may be used immediately, or frozen for use in the winter.

Mix lamb, rice, butter, allspice, salt and pepper and water. Lay the leaves flat on the table and take 1 tsp of the mixture (depending on how large the leaves are) and put in a row in the leaves.

Turn the sides of the leaves inward and roll up like a "cigar." They should be loosely rolled to leave room for the rice to expand.

Remove the water from the lamb bone. Arrange grape leaves around the bone and when finished, cover with a heavy dish. Add the lamb water and cover.

Cook for approximately 30-40 minutes.

TIP: Grape leaves can be blanched and kept in refrigerator for 1 week prior to using. After they are rolled they can be put in the freezer for future use. You can also freeze the leaves by themselves and roll when ready to use.

Kefta (Lamburgers)

This is a summertime barbeque favorite, but can be broiled in the oven all year.

    1 lb. finely ground extra lean lamb.   1 tsp Allspice
    1 onion finely chopped   ½ cup chopped parsley

Mix all ingredients, add salt and pepper to taste, and form links about ½ the size of a frankfurter. Cook on barbeque for 2-4 minutes on each side depending on whether you like rare, medium or well done.

Loobie and Rice, (String Beans and Rice)

This is almost like a stew and cooked today by many people of all nationalities!

It's a healthy dish that can be kept for a week as leftovers. It can also be altered by using peas or mushrooms or both rather than stringbeans.

1 lb. cubed lamb or beef	salt and pepper
2 boxes frozen string beans	1 cup vermacelli noodles
1 large clove garlic	2 cups rice
1 tbsp onion flakes	1 stick butter
1 can whole tomatoes	

Saute meat with ½ stick butter, sales and pepper for approximately 15-20 minutes. Add stringbeans, tomatoes, garlic and onion flakes and 2 cups water. Cook on medium flame for 1 ½ hours.

Saute balance of butter with vermicelli noodles until they are brown. Add three cups of water and two cups of rice. Cover and cook on medium heat until rice is tender.

Koosa (Stuffed Zuccini)

This is a warm favorite of just about all Middle Eastern descent people.

6 medium size zuccini	¾ lb ground lamb or beef
1 cup rice	½ stick butter
1 can or 6 fresh tomatoes	2 cups water
salt and pepper	1 large clove garlic
allspice	

A zuccini scraper can be purchased in any Middle East store. Carefully scrape out each zuccini (put scrapings aside for Mfarakee. See meatless dishes) Mix meat, butter rice and salt and pepper/allspice. Fill each zucchini and arrange in pot. Pour all other ingredients including salt and pepper and cook for approximately 35 minutes on medium flame.

Malfoof (Rolled Cabbage)

This is one of my favorites. Use the same ingredients as Grape Leaves filling.

Cut cabbage in half and boil until the leaves are tender. After it has cooled, remove each leaf and roll and fill with rice stuffing.

This should be arranged in layers in a pot with lemon and a few cloves of garlic or with a tomato sauce for which you would use the Koosa recipe.

Shash Barak (Middle East dumplings in Yogurt)

This recipe is a lot of work, but if you are a yogurt lover – it is well worth preparing. The dumplings can be frozen for later use.

1 cup flour	½ lb chopped lamb
¼ cup onions	all spice
3 cups plain Yogurt	1 clove mashed garlic
½ cup dried mint	½ cup rice
½ cup water (approx.)	2 tbsp butter
salt and pepper	

Mix flour and water until dough is pliable for rolling. Mix lamb and onion with butter. Roll dough very thin and cut into circles with a glass. Take a small piece of the meat mixture and put in the middle of the dough.

Wrap one side of the dough over the other and crimp around the outside. Take a piece of the filled dough between your thumb and forefinger and wrap it around to meet the other side until it forms a dumpling. Bake on buttered baking dish until the   dough turns light brown.

In a saucepan add the yogurt, dried mint and mashed garlic **constantly stirring** until the mixture begins to simmer. Add the rice and continue simmering. You may need to add a small amount of water. Once the mixture comes to a boil, add the dumplings and cook the rice until finished.

This is a lot of work and you really have to love it to make it. I usually freeze some of the dumplings – but I only cook it once or twice a year.

Stuffed Eggplant

This recipe is also a favorite with many people.

<table>
<tr><td>1 large eggplant</td><td>¾ lb lamb or beef</td></tr>
<tr><td>1/8 cup pignolia nuts</td><td>1/8 lb butter</td></tr>
<tr><td>onion flakes</td><td>salt and pepper/allspice</td></tr>
</table>

1 can tomato paste mixed with water, oregano, basil, salt and pepper, garlic and onion flakes.

Peel and cut salted eggplant into 8 pieces. Pierce side and bake in oven at 350 degrees for approximately 40 minutes until tender. While eggplant is baking, lightly sauté meat onions and pignolia nuts in butter, add salt and pepper/allspice.

Spoon a full tablespoon into pierced eggplant pieces. Pour tomato sauce over mixture and bake for 35 minutes. This is normally served with our special rice. See side dishes.

NOTES

Entrees –
American, Italian
and other

Entrees American, Italian and other

Beef Stew

A winter time favorite. Any vegetable can be added, but this is the recipe I use.

    1 cup fresh mushrooms or 1 jar 1 cup chopped celery
    1 lb. cubed chuck or sirloin   1 cup chopped carrots
    4 medium potatoes cut in half 1 can peas
    1 cup balsamic vinegar   1 bay leaf
    1 onion   3 cups water

Salt and pepper meat and dip in flour. Brown meat in butter and oil and add balsamic vinegar and add water and all other ingredients. Wondra or any other Flour can be added to make the gravy a little thicker. If gravy is not dark enough, add Gravy Master. Cook on moderate heat for approximately 1 ½ hrs or until meat is tender.

Chicken, Chicken, Chicken and of course, Turkey

TIP: Always wash, salt and pepper chicken or indeed any poultry one day prior to cooking. It is far more flavorful and totally devoid of bacteria.

There are literally hundreds of ways to cook chicken, but by far, Southern Fried Chicken is the chicken of choice for most people. The basic recipe was handed down to me by my father and my mother and I have varied it in many ways through the years.

Many people serve fried chicken with honey. We discovered this delicious secret on our honeymoon in Montreal – so many years ago!

TIP: Oil used for frying can be reused. Just strain and put away in a glass jar. The oil tastes better with each use. Add new oil as needed.

Basic Southern Fried Chicken

This is by far everyone's favorite!

    Several pieces of Chicken–your choice
    salt and pepper   1" oil in fry pan   flour

Mix salt and pepper and flour together and dip each piece of chicken into the mixture.

Heat oil on moderate flame and then add chicken and cover for approximately 10 minutes. Remove cover and turn chicken over and cook for another 10 minutes uncovered until be browned. Place on paper towels to remove excess oil and serve.

Variation 2 Southern Fried Chicken

Same as above, but a small dish of milk is required.

Dip chicken in milk prior to dipping into the flour mixture. This creates a crispier coating to the chicken.

Variation 3 Southern Fried Chicken

Same as above, but add breadcrumbs and grated cheese and whipped egg with milk.

Mix breadcrumbs (either plain or flavored) together with grated cheese. Dip chicken in flour mixture, followed by dipping in whipped egg, followed by dipping into the breadcrumb mixture.

For a less fattening meal – but still very tasty – place a small amount of oil on a baking sheet and bake at 350 degrees for 40 minutes. Turn over and cook for another 25 minutes to brown the second side.

Chicken Nuggets and/or Chicken Strips

For this we use only white meat chicken. Cut the nuggets into small pieces less than the size of a ping pong ball. For strips, you can use Chicken Tenders or Breast of Chicken and slice into strips.

For a party as an appetizer, chicken nuggets should be prepared according to variation 3. I usually serve this with a honey mustard sauce – which is 1/3 honey and 2/3 mustard. Chicken strips were originally made for the young children in the family – but most times, the adults enjoy them as much as the children. It's always been a favorite of my nieces and nephews, Alex, Julia, Katie, Ryan, Alyssa and Brandon – and will certainly be a favorite of James, Nicole and Sean in the next few years. They too, are best prepared according to variation 3 and normally served with whatever we have for dinner.

TIP: Spices create delicious flavor in many Middle Eastern dishes. Our primary spice is allspice in many of our foods.

Chicken (Middle Eastern Style)

These are the basic spices we use for both chicken and turkey when roasting.

1 chicken cut up in pieces	allspice, cinnamon
1 tbsp butter	sage, poultry seasoning
salt and pepper	

Apply spices to chicken parts, allspice, cinnamon, salt and pepper, poultry seasoning and sage and cover with bits of butter. If possible, apply spices the day prior to cooking. Cover and cook for one hour at 400 degrees. Brown uncovered at 425 degrees for 15 minutes.

Chicken Cacciatore

This delicious Italian recipe is a variation of the original but we feel it tastes just as good

.chicken parts
1 can tomato paste
salt and pepper
2 slices bacon

1 sliced onion
3 cups water
bay leaf

Fry bacon until crisp in olive oil. Remove and fry chicken parts until browned. Add tomato paste, water, onion and bay leaf onion. Crumble bacon and cook until chicken is tender. Variations can include string beans, potatoes, peas, mixed vegetables or whatever you like!

Stuffed Breast of Chicken

This is one of my favorite chicken recipes. It can be altered in many ways. You can cook it dry rather than with a gravy, or you can add a little lemon juice or other spices such as oregano, basil, garlic. It comes out pretty good no matter how you make it.

6 boneless chicken breasts
¾ cup grated cheese
½ lb mozzarella
3 tbsp olive oil
3 tbsp butter

¼ cup milk
1 jar mushrooms
¾ cup bread crumbs
Wondra Flour

Salt and pepper chicken one day ahead. Mix grated cheese and bread crumbs – set aside half – mix other half with mozzarella. Dip breasts into milk and stuff with mozzarella mixture. Bread chicken with balance and arrange in baking dish with olive oil. Sprinkle Wondra and butter over each piece. Bake at 350 for approx 30 minutes. Add 1 cup water and mushrooms and bake for 15 minutes. You may need to add 1 chicken bullion cube and salt and pepper to taste. Can be served with potatoes, rice or pasta.

Chicken Parmagina

This is most everyone's favorite – except for those who eat veal. This recipe can be used for either one.

    1 lb. thin sliced breast   1 cup bread crumbs
    ½ cup grated cheese   1 egg
    ¼ cup milk   salt and pepper
    ¼ cup flour (optional)   ¼ cup oil

Salt and pepper chicken the day before. Mix bread crumbs (flavored or plain) and grated cheese

Whip egg and add milk. Dip chicken in flour and then into egg mixture followed by breadcrumb mixture. Dip each piece in oil in pan and turn over. Cook for approximately 20-30 minutes at 350 until brown.

Add sauce (see recipe) and top with slices or shredded mozzarella cheese and bake for 5-10 minutes more.

Lemon Chicken

Prepare chicken for parmigianaa. Rather than adding sauce, etc, apply a tablespoon of lemon juice on each slice of chicken. Bake an additional ten minutes until golden brown.

Chicken Casserole

This is another of Lorraine's great recipes that I have never really mastered but mine still tastes pretty good!

    3 boneless chicken breasts   ½ lb Velveeta cheese
    1 pkg egg noodles   ½ lb. cheddar cheese
    1 pkg carrots(cubed   1 cup milk
    bread crumbs/croutons   ½ stick butter
    6-8 stalks celery (cut into cubes).
    red roasted pepper cut into cubes

Boil chicken with celery and carrots and butter until well cooked. Remove chicken and cut into cubes. Add chicken, noodles and cook for 10 minutes. Add cheeses and milk and salt and pepper to taste, stirring constantly. Pour into baking dish and cover with buttered bread crumbs or croutons. Bake for approximately one half hour.

Dad's Marinated Chicken

My father originated this recipe which has been enjoyed by our family and others for many years. It's great to serve at a barbeque and is prepared in advance.

8-10 chicken parts	¾ cup balsamic vinegar
1 large clove garlic	½ cup lemon juice
½ cup olive or canola oil	salt/pepper

Wash chicken the day before. Cut garlic in quarters. Add all ingredients and let marinate overnight. The next day, barbeque chicken turning after a few minutes on high. The chicken should only cook for 10 minutes. Remove and put back into the marinade and simmer on medium heat for 2 – 3 hours and serve.

My Marinated Chicken

This is very similar to Dad's chicken but some people do not like the flavor of garlic so I have altered it a bit.

8-10 chicken parts	½ cup lemon juice
½ cup olive oil	salt/pepper

¾ cup Wishbone Balsamic Vinegar

Wash chicken and add all ingredients. Remove the oil from the Wishbone Dressing and replace with olive oil. Follow balance of instructions on Dad's Chicken. Both these recipes can also be cooked in the oven in the winter. Cook at 400 covered and lower to 350 covered for two hours.

Chicken Oreganato

This Italian favorite will almost certainly make your mouth water.

8-10 pieces chicken	½ cup breadcrumbs
1 tsp oregano	1 tsp basil
1 tsp parsley	½ tsp garlic salt
¼ cup lemon juice	½ cup olive oil

Arrange chicken on baking sheet. Mix breadcrumbs, oregano, basil, parsley and garlic salt. Spread mixture over the chicken. Mix lemon juice and olive oil and drizzle over chicken. Bake covered for 45 minutes at 350. Uncover for 15 minutes more. Some people like more lemon – so feel free to add. You may also use flavored breadcrumbs.

Shrimp Oreganato

Another Italian favorite that is enjoyed by many.

8-10 pieces chicken	½ cup breadcrumbs
1 tsp oregano	1 tsp basil
1 tsp parsley	½ tsp garlic salt
¼ cup lemon juice	½ cup olive oil

Arrange cooked shrimp on baking sheet. Mix breadcrumbs, oregano, basil, parsley and garlic salt. Spread mixture over the chicken. Mix lemon juice and olive oil and drizzle over chicken. Bake covered for 20 at 350. Add more lemon if desired – so feel free to add. You may also use flavored breadcrumbs.

Baked Fish

This recipe I make with sole. It is simple and tastes wonderful. You can use other kinds of fish if you like.

1 lb. filet of sole	½ cup milk
½ cup breadcrumbs	lemon juice
oregano, basil, parsley,	½ cup olive oil
¼ cup grated cheese	salt and pepper

Mix breadcrumbs, basil, oregano, parsley and grated cheese. Salt and pepper fish, dip in milk and then dip in breadcrumb mixture. Cover bottom of 9 x 12 pan with olive oil. Place fish on olive oil and flip over so the fish is covered in oil. Bake in 350 over for 15 minutes. Add 1 teaspoon of lemon juice on to each piece of fish and cook for another 15 minutes.

TIP: Flavored breadcrumbs can be used in most all recipes calling for oregano, basil and parsley.

Meatballs

This is my basic recipe which can be altered to your own taste. It can be used alone or with Italian sauce.

1 lb. chopped beef	½ cup grated cheese
1 egg	½ cup water
1 cup bread crumbs	1 tbsp onion flakes

Mix all ingredients – you may have to add a little water to have a softer consistency to the meatballs. Form meatballs the size of a golf ball, unless you are making Lasaga or Baked Ziti or Penne, then form small balls the size of a large marble. To this recipe, you can add, sausage, pieces of beef or pork or veal.

Sauce–Italian (for making spaghetti, lasagna, etc.)

There are plenty of store-bought sauces, but it always tastes better home made.

1 tbsp dry onions	1 clove garlic
¼ cup olive oil.	1 can crushed, whole, or pureed tomatoes
1 can of tomato paste	1 tsp oregano
1 tsp basil	1 tsp parsley
salt and pepper	1 tsp baking soda optional

Saute onions and garlic in cup olive oil. Add crushed, whole, or pureed tomatoes and tomato paste. Add oregano, basil, parsley, salt and pepper. This can cook for one hour to ten hours. I usually cook about two hours. It's the basic sauce I use and to this meatballs, sausage, pork, veal or beef may be added.

Sausage and Peppers

This goes with almost all Italian or American barbeques.

1 lb Italian sausages	3 green/red pepper
1 large sliced onion	1 tbsp Worcestershire Sauce
salt and pepper	4 tbsp olive oil

Brown sausages in olive oil. Slice onion and pepper and add other ingredients. Cook on medium heat until sausage in ready – about 35 minutes. Sausage can be sliced into pieces or length wise.

Spareribs Barbequed

This recipe is actually baked, but the first time I tried it, it was called barbecued. It can be barbequed and placed back in the sauce several times until tender. You be the judge

1 can tomato sauce	2 lbs pork spareribs
1 tbsp Worcestershire Sauce	¼ cup vinegar
2 tbsp olive oil	1 tbsp chopped onions
2 cups water	salt and pepper

Mix all ingredients and pour over spareribs in baking dish. Cook at 350 for approximately 2 hours turning two or three times.

Peppers - Stuffed

See Koosa (stuffed zucchini) same recipe except replace garlic in tomato sauce with sliced onion.

TIP: A teaspoon of baking soda makes tomato sauce a little less acidy.

Ziti/Lasagna Baked

This is a favorite of most all families. Can be served immediately or frozen for future use.

1 lb. ricotta	1 egg	1 box ziti or lasagna
½ lb. mozzarella		½ cup grated cheese

Sauce used for spaghetti, but meatballs the size of a large marble.

Mix ricotta, mozzarella, grated cheese and egg. cook ziti or lasagna in salted water. Layer the sauce, then the ziti, add the ricotta mixture and then sauce and repeat

Top with shredded mozzarella and bake covered for 1 hour at 350 degrees. Let cool for 20 minutes before serving.

Pesto Sauce

This is one of my favorite sauces for gnocci or rigatoni and can be used with just about any pasta – if you like it!

2 cups minced fresh basil	1 ½ cups olive oil
¼ cup mashed pignolia nuts	3 cloves mashed garlic
¾ cup grated cheese	1 tsp salt

Mix all ingredients in food processor and serve. Can be refrigerated up to two weeks or frozen for later use.

Swedish Meatballs

This recipe can be used as a main course with vegetables and potatoes or as an appetizer.

½ lb chopped sirloin	½ lb. chopped pork
¼ cup grated cheese	1 cup breadcrumbs
¼ cup flour	1 can mushrooms
1 tbsp onion flakes	

Mix all ingredients (some prefer all beef so double beef, others also add veal. Form balls into a little smaller than a ping pong ball. Again, you may have to add water. Fry with olive oil and two tbsp butter. Can be served dry or you can add some Wondra, gravy master, a bay leaf and water to enjoy the meatballs in a brown gravy.

Pizza Rustica

This is a traditional Italian Easter Breakfast dish – but most eat it any time. It is delicious but I do not cook it more than once a year. It's a heart attack waiting to happen but so delectable.

1 dozen raw eggs	1 dozen hard boiled eggs
½ lb. prosciutto	½ lb. ham
½ lb. capicolla	2 lbs. mozzarella
1 lb. swiss cheese	½ lb dried sausage
½ lb. salami	½ lb. supersod

Crust

2 cups flour	¾ cup Crisco
1 – 1 ½ cup warm water	salt and pepper

Mix all crust ingredients until firm. Do not put too much water. Dough should be pliable. Roll out and cover bottom and sides of 9 x 13 pan or two cake pans – keeping enough dough to cover the pie.

Slice up all meats and cheese. Put hard boiled eggs through egg cutter. Mix all meats and cheese together with 1 dozen raw eggs. Layer hard boiled eggs over the crust. Cover eggs with meat mixture and add another layer of eggs and mixture until there is no more left. Cover entire pie with layer of dough. With your hand, pat top of pie with thin layer of milk. Put a few holes with a fork on top to allow the filling to breath.

Bake for approximately 1 ½ hours at 350. Toothpick should come out clean!

Shrimp–Fried

This is so easy to make and so utterly delicious to eat.

1 lb. shrimp	½ cup flour
1 egg	1 tsp baking powder
½ cup water	salt and pepper
olive oil	

Mix all ingredients except shrimp and olive oil, until creamy. Heat oil in fry pan until hot. Dip shrimp in mixture and fry on each side for just one minute until browned. For tartar sauce mix ½ cup mayonnaise with 1 tablespoon relish.

Pot Roast

My pot roast recipe is similar to beef stew – except use rump roast and cook for approximately 2 – 2 ½ hours.

Virginia Ham

Ed's grandmother taught me to cook a ham this way. It's easy and delicious – and healthier since a lot of the salt is removed by boiling.

½ ham	1 can pineapple halves
cherries	1 cup brown sugar
½ cup water	4 tbsp mustard
1 tsp cloves	

Boil ham in pot of water for approximately ½ hour. Remove from heat. Brush with mustard. Apply pineapple halves to top of ham and put a cherry in each. Mix brown sugar and water together and pour over ham. Insert cloves around the ham. Cook at 350 for approximately 1 hour.

NOTES

Side Dishes
Meatless

Bread Dressing for Chicken or Turkey

This is our basic recipe that we always use. Some people add their own ingredients like eggs, sausage but this is the only recipe I use.

1 medium loaf toasted white bread   1 stick butter
½ quart milk (approximately) 1 small chopped onion
1 tsp sage   1 tsp poultry seasoning
1 tsp allspice   1 ½ cups chopped celery

Saute onion and celery together with all spices in sauce pan until celery is soft. Break up toasted bread into small pieces. Mix everything together and slowly add the milk. It should not be dry, you may need to add a little more milk. When it is all fairly wet, stuff the poultry and cook covered at 350. How long the cooking takes depends on how large the poultry. Normally, we cook it 25 minutes per pound when it is stuffed. This dressing can also be baked on its own.

Manicotti

Mother and I spent many a day making these. I think I'm just getting too lazy to make them today.

4 eggs   1 cup flour
dash of salt   1 cup warm water

Stuffing

1 lb ricotta   ½ lb. mozzarella cheese shredded
1 egg   ½ cup grated cheese

Mix all ingredients together and pour about 2 tablespoons into a moderately heated fry pan – do not allow to brown. Simply fry on one side until fairly dry.

Fill each with one tablespoon stuffing, roll. Apply tomato sauce to bottom of pan and place manicotti on baking sheet.

Cover each one with a small amount of sauce and bake for approximately 20-30 minutes.

Mjadarah – Lentils and Rice

Both Mother and Lorraine's Mjadarah is hard to master, but I try my best and this recipe comes somewhere near theirs!

1 bag lentils	2 cups rice
3 sliced onions crisply fried	1/2 cup olive oil
salt and pepper	

Cook Lentils and Rice, salt and pepper with approximately 3-4 cups water over medium heat. While this is cooking, fry onions in olive oil with salt and pepper. Remove from heat on paper towel. When lentils and rice are soft (approx. 25 minutes)., drain excess water and add olive oil from fried onions and stir. Top with fried onions. This is a warm favorite that can be served hot, cold or at room temperature. It was originally a Lebanese Lenten dish served with mixed salad or cole slaw but has now become a popular Friday treat.

Mfarakee (Zucchini)

When making Koosa (stuffed zucchini) the inside cannot be wasted – it's too delicious. Use this recipe if you use eight zucchinis – for less, use less condiments.

zucchini stuffing	3 fresh tomatoes
1 tbsp onion	2 tbsp olive oil
1 tbsp butter	salt and pepper

Mix all ingredients and cook over medium flame until tender. This can be eaten as a side dish or as a breakfast treat if you add eggs and mix with zucchini after it is cooked. Some people also add chopped beef or lamb to make it a main course. Others omit the tomatoes.

Rice and Noodles

This particular rice is used with Looby and Rice and the many variations of it. Many people enjoy the rice plain or with a dollop of yogurt over it.

1 cup rice	½ cup Vermacelli noodles
1/8 lb butter	2 cups water

Saute noodles in butter until golden brown. Add water and rice and simmer for approximately 20 minutes until rice is cooked.

Spinach

This is a great Lenten dish – goes particularly well with pita bread. Can also be used as a side dish or a nice meatless lunch!

2 boxes frozen or 2 bags fresh spinach   salt and pepper
¼ cup lemon juice (to taste)   ¼ cup olive oil
1 tsp onion flakes or chopped onion
3 onions sliced and fried for topping (optional)

Cook spinach in fry pan for just a few moments and mix in all other ingredients. Top with crisply fried onions.

String Beans/Tomatoes

Another delicious Lent or side dish which is the same ingredients as Looby and Rice, but meatless.

1 clove garlic   ¼ cup olive oil
1 bag frozen or 1 lb fresh string beans
3 fresh tomatoes or 1 sm can tomato sauce
1 tbsp onion flakes or 1 small onion
salt and pepper to taste.

Mix all ingredients and cook over medium flame for approximately 30-40 minutes until beans become soft.

Side Dishes
Meat

Chili Con Carne

This is another addition to a great barbeque.

1 ½ lbs. ground chuck/sirloin	2 tbsp chili powder
2 cans kidney beans	4 tbsp olive oil
1 large clove garlic mashed	2 tbsp cumin powder
1 medium can tomato sauce	1 green pepper cubed
1 hot pepper finely chopped	

Saute meat together and then add all ingredients until peppers are soft except the beans. Mix in the beans and cook for approximately ½ hour.

You can add cheese or sour cream topping or oyster crackers for a delicious touch.

Dad's Famous Hot Dog Chili

This was my father's secret recipe and I now give it to all of you to carry on. It has become a tradition to make this at barbeques to put on frankfurters.

1 lb. ground chuck or sirloin	1 clove mashed garlic
2 tsp. chili powder	2 tsp cumin powder
2 tbsp olive oil	2 tbsp tomato sauce
salt and pepper	

Sauté meat and garlic in olive oil making sure particles of meat are separated. Meat should be fine rather than coarse. Taste to ensure seasoning is right. Add all other ingredients and serve.

Fried Rice

The first time Ed and I tried to cook fried rice, it did not occur to us that we had to boil the rice. We tried to cook it in vain for two hours and then went out to eat.

2 cups boiled rice	4 tbsp soy sauce
1 pc. pork, chicken or shrimp cubed	2 eggs
4 tbsp olive oil	1 onion
1 cup vegetables (mixed, peas, or whatever you like)	

Boil rice in 4 cups of water. Saute pork and onion until cooked. Add rice, vegetables and soy sauce stirring. Mix eggs thoroughly and drizzle over mixture.

To make this an entrée – use more pork, chicken or shrimp.

Rice Dressing for Chicken or Turkey

The quantity depends on how many you are cooking for. This recipe is for around 4 people

1 cup rice	½ lb. chopped lamb
5 tbsp butter	1 tsp allspice
½ cup chicken broth or two chicken boullion cubes	

Topping:

1/8 lb. butter	¼ cup pignolia nuts
1/8 cup slivered almonds	salt and pepper

Saute lamb in butter together with other ingredients (beef may be used, but lamb is more flavorful) Add two cups of water and rice and rice and simmer on medium flame until rice is fluffy. This can then either be stuffed into the chicken or turkey or can be served as is.

While rice is simmering, sauté nuts in butter until brown. Put rice on serving place and pour nut mixture over the entire top.

NOTES

Middle East Desserts

Middle East Desserts

TIP: Almost any strange sounding ingredient can be purchased in all Middle Eastern or Greek shops.

Baklava

This dessert in our culture is usually made at Christmas – but it is enjoyed by most all year long.

> 1 box phyllo dough   1 lb. butter
> 3 tbsp rose water (Mazahar) ¾ cup sugar
> 2 cups chopped pistachios or walnuts

Topping

> 1 ½ cups sugar   3 cups water
> 2 tbsp rose water

Melt Butter. Mix nuts, sugar and Rose Water. Line bottom of 9 x 12 pan with butter using a pastry brush – or the old fashioned way, with your hands. Layer half of the phyllo dough, one at a time, buttering each layer. Pat down the nut mixture and layer second half buttering each layer.

Let harden a few minutes in the refrigerator. Remove and cut into triangles with a very sharp knife. Bake in over at 325 for approximately one hour or until the dough is lightly browned. Remove from oven and cool for an hour or so. Pour topping over the entire tray.

Caak Shami

This is a favorite coffee or tea snack. I personally love it for breakfast – as do my brothers and many of my nieces and nephews.

> 5 cups flour   4 cups milk   ½ lb. Crisco
> 3 cups sugar   ½ lb. Butter   ½ cup oil
> ½ cup anise seed   3 packets yeast 1 tsp salt
> 3 tbsp Hab't il barakee (black fennel seeds)

Topping

| 2 eggs | ½ cup milk | 2 tbsp sugar |

Melt butter and Crisco and mix all ingredients. Let stand covered, until dough rises for about two hours. Take one sixth of the dough and roll out with hands on flat surface. Cut rolled dough into pieces a little larger than a ping pong ball. Roll each piece into a strip and form dough into eights and 0's. Arrange on baking sheet. Mix eggs, sugar and milk and brush each with mixture. Bake at 350 degrees for 12-15 minutes until brown.

Caak Ab Haleeb (Easter Cakes)

This is a warm favorite of the whole family. When my brothers and his family come to visit we always have a large quantity on hand. They can eat these for breakfast, lunch, dinner or a snack.

5 cups flour	4 cups milk
3 cups sugar	½ lb. butter
½ lb. Crisco	½ cup oil
1 tsp baking powder	1 tsp salt
3 tbsp hab't il barakee (black fennel seeds)	
½ cup anise seed	3 packets yeast
1 tsp Mahlab	cut glass dish

Dip

| 2 cups milk | two tbsp corn starch |
| 2 tbsp rosewater | 1 cup sugar |

Melt butter and Crisco and mix all ingredients. Let stand covered, until dough rises for about two hours. Mix all the dipping ingredients over a medium flame until sugar is dissolved and it begins to simMer. You can substitute rosewater with vanilla Extract.

Take one sixth of the dough and roll out with hands on flat surface. Cut rolled dough into pieces between a ping pong ball and a tennis ball. Roll each piece into a ball and when finished take each one and press onto back side of cut glass dish, to create a design.

Put on baking sheet and let the stand five minutes. Bake at 350 degrees for approximately 15 minutes, starting at bottom of oven and putting on top for half the time in order to brown. Dip each cake into the milk mixture and stand on side until they dry.

Date Cookies

Date cookies are my son's favorite dessert – My sister made a package each year for him at Christmas. He was so delighted.

    1 cup ground dates   1/3 cup finely chopped walnuts
    4 tbsp butter

Same as Mamool except substitute nut mixture Roll dates out into cigar shapes, insert into the dough and flap over. Decorate once again with fork.

Mahmool

Same recipe as shortbread – except add ¼ cup more flour.

 Stuffing:

    1 cup chopped walnuts, pecans or pistachios
    ¾ cup sugar   1 tbsp rosewater

Pat cookies between hands to fit the palm of the hand. Add 1 tablespoon stuffing mixture and roll into ball. Decorate with a fork making designs

Bake for 10 15 minutes at 350 degrees.

Shortbread - Middle Eastern

This is probably one of the best loved cookies we make. It melts in your mouth.

    1 cup melted sweet butter   ¾ cup sugar
    2¾ cups flour   1 tbsp vanilla or rosewater extract
    Optional: almond halves peeled

Beat butter with a hand mixer until it becomes light and fluffy. Add vanilla and sugar and beat again slowly adding the flour until the dough is soft and pliable. Roll dough with hand and form 'S' and 'O' shapes on cookie sheet. Apply almond half to each cookie. Bake at 450 degrees for approximately 10 minutes. Do not allow the cookies to brown.

Pancakes/Ricotta

This is my sister-in-law's favorite Middle Eastern dessert. It's a lot of work – but the taste is well worth it!

Pancakes

1 cup flour   ¾ cup sugar
4 tbsp Oil   1 tsp Vanila
1 cup milk

Stuffing:

½ lb ricotta   ¼ lb mozzarella cheese
½ cup sugar   1 egg

Topping:

1 cup sugar   1 tbsp tose water
1 ½ cups water

Mix all pancake ingredients – then mix all stuffing ingredients.

Cook topping over moderate heat until sugar is dissolved. Pour 2 tablespoons of pancake batter into warm fry pan on moderate heat. When bubbles begin to form remove from heat and put one tablespoon of stuffing on top of pancake

and close and crimp all sides. Repeat this until all pancakes are completed.

Melt butter in frying pan on moderate heat. Fry pancake
for one minute on each side. Remove from heat and serve
with Sugar Topping.

American Desserts

American Desserts

TIP: To test cakes, when almost baked, place a toothpick in the center. The cake is finished if the toothpick come out clean.

Chocolate Cake

There are many wonderful cake mixes on the market today – but it is difficult to beat a homemade chocolate cake.

2 cups sugar	½ cup shortening
3 eggs	2 sq. unsweetened chocolate
3 cups flour	1 tsp baking powder
1 cup buttermilk*	1 tsp vanilla
1 cup hot water.	

*add 1 tsp white vinegar to 1 cup of milk to make your own Buttermilk.

Cream sugar, butter and eggs with mixer until fluffy. Add all other ingredients and place in 9 x 12 buttered and floured pan. Bake at 375 for approximately 40 minutes. Ice when cool.

Cream Puffs

Is there anyone who doesn't like cream puffs?

1 cup water	1 cup flour
½ cup shortening	4 large eggs
¼ tsp sale	

Heat water, shortening and salt to full rolling boil. Reduce heat and quickly stir in flour. Vigorously mix until mixture leaves side of pan. Remove from heat and add eggs – one at a time and mix well until smooth.

Drop spoon of dough onto greased cooking sheet. Bake at 450 degrees for 10 minutes and then lower to 350 and bake for 25 minutes until golden brown. Cut in half while hot and return to open oven

Cream filling

3 cups milk	½ cup sugar
4 eggs	5 tbsp corn starch

Stir sugar and milk over moderate heat and remove when it comes to a boil. Mix egg yolks well and add with cornstarch to mixture.

Fill cream puffs with one tablespoon of the mixture and serve. For variations, you can fill with whipped cream, chocolate cream, or ice cream.

Pineapple Upside Down Cake

This was my Mother's recipe and I never found another that equaled it!

2 cups flour	½ cup butter
1 cup sugar	1 cup pineapple juice
3 Tsp Baking Powder	2 eggs
½ Tsp salt	

Bottom Layer

¼ lb butter	2 cups brown sugar
1 can pineapple cut in rounds	

Mix all ingredients about 300 strokes by hand or one minute by mixer. Dissolve ¼ lb butter with two cups brown sugar and spread on bottom or pan. Arrange pineapple over brown sugar. Pour dough over mixture and bake at 350 degrees for 30 – 35 minutes. It's optional but you can add cherries inside each of the pineapple rings and walnuts around the bottom before baking.

Pound Cake

This recipe was handed down by many generations of Ed's relatives. His Aunt Carrie passed it on to me and it's the best pound cake ever! It tastes better each day and keeps up to two weeks.

½ lb. butter	½ cup milk
2 cups sugar	½ tsp vanilla
6 eggs	½ tsp lemon
3 cups flour	3 tsp baking powder
½ tsp salt	

Combine and blend butter and sugar, add eggs and mix thoroughly, add all other ingredients and pour into deep buttered and floured baking pan. Bake at 350 for approximately one hour.

This cake has many variations:

1.	Mix half the dough with two packets of chocolate and pour into baking dish for a marble cake.
2.	Use orange juice rather than milk and scrape rind of orange for a delicious orange cake.
3.	Add either white or chocolate icing.
4.	Mix sugar and cinnamon combined with walnuts into the mixture for coffee cake.
5.	Make up your own new recipe!

Basic Pie Crust

This was our family recipe for never fail pie dough. It was always delicious and many thousands of pies were baked with this recipe.

6 cups flour	1 tsp salt
1 lb Crisco	2 tbsp sugar

Mix all ingredients until pliable. Roll out dough and put into pie dish. This will make three double piecrusts or six open crusts. This basic crust can be used for any type of pie.

For uncovered pies, the crust must be backed for about 20 minutes in advance and let cool before adding mixture.

Apple Pie

Ah - the staple of American Pies. And nothing tastes better than a home made one!

12 apples peeled cored and sliced   ½ cup sugar
2 tbsp Cinnamon   ¼ cup raisins
½ cup milk

Mix all ingredients and pour into crust. Cover pie with second crust layer and make holes with fork on the pie. Pour a small amount of milk into your hand and apply to top of pie for a shine on the finished product. Bake for approximately 35 – 40 minutes until crust is slightly browned.

Thanksgiving Pumpkin Pie

Everyone has always loved my mother's pies. This is wonderful.

2 cups pumpkin cooked ½ cup sugar
½ tsp salt   3 eggs
2 cups scalded milk   1 tsp cinnamon
½ tsp ginger   ½ tsp Allspice
½ tsp nutmet   ¼ tsp mace

Combine well beaten egg yolks, ¼ cup sugar, salt and spices. Stir in milk and pumpkin gradually. Beat remaining sugar into stiffly beaten egg whites. Fold into pumpkin mixture. Pour into crust and bake at 450 degrees for 30 40 minutes. Put knife into pie and when it comes out clean, pie is done.

Now this was Mother's original recipe. For those who prefer the easy way use canned pumpkin. Use instructions on can, but it always tastes best when you add above quantities of allspice, nutmeg and cinnamon to mixture

Pecan Pie

This is one of my all time favorites. I have never seen Mother's recipe duplicated by anyone.

6 egg whites	2 cups chopped pecans
1 pint white corn syrup	7 tbsps butter
1 box shredded coconut	2 tsp vanilla
6 tbsp sugar	pinch of salt

Mix pecans, coconut, sugar, flour. Add syrup eggs, butter,. Do not mix too much. Line 9 x 12 tray with pie dough. Bake 35 minutes at 375 degrees, then 10 minutes at 300. Cut when cool.

Brownies

My sister, Lorraine, gave me this recipe so many years ago – and it is absolutely delicious every time! It is the best!!

4 squares unsweetened chocolate	½ cup butter
2 cups sugar	4 eggs
1 cup flour	1 tsp vanilla
1 cup walnuts or pecans (optional)	

Mix all ingredients coarsely (do not whip) and bake at 375 for approximately 40 minutes.

Miscellaneous

Miscellaneous

Leban (Yogurt) and Lebanee (Yogurt Cheese)

Fresh yogurt cannot be made without a culture so you must buy a small plain yogurt to start. Lebanee is a delicious creamy cheese that is normally eaten at breakfast with black olives and pita bread. I love it with zatar.

2 tbsp yogurt   1 quart milk   1 tsp salt

Combine all ingredients until just before it comes to a boil. Remove from heat and completely cover with a large towel. Let sit for at least 8 hours and refrigerate. Do not use until the next day.

To make Lebanee, pour yogurt into a gauze bag or place in a strainer. Add salt according to taste. Let sift for 2 – 3 hours at room temperature and then place in refrigerator. Both stay fresh for many weeks.

Syrian Cheese

This is a light cheese that is normally served as an appetizer in a Lebanese home. It is also eaten at breakfast with pita bread.

1 gallon milk   4 gelatin tablets   1 cup coarse salt

Bring milk to a simmer, remove from heat and crush tablets and let cool slightly. When you can put your pinky into the milk for a count of ten, stir in the crushed gelatin. Let sit for about ½ hour.

Put both hands into the mixture and start draining passing from hamd to hand forming a circular disc. After cool, mix salt in 2 quart of water. Put cheese into the refrigerator. The may be kept for many months, but when you are ready to eat, it will be very salty, so you must run under water for several minutes.

INDEX

-A-

Antipasto Tray 54

-B-

Baba Ghanoush 55
Baklava 106
Beef Stew 86
Bread Dressing 98
Breakfast Quiche 50
Broccoli Casserole 55

-C-

Caak Shami 106
Caak Ab Haleeb 107
Cakes:
    Pineapple Upside
      Down 113
    Pound Cake 114
    Chocolate 112
Cheesebread 56
Chicken:
    Basic Southern Fried . 87
    Var. 2 Southern Fried . 87
    Var. 3 Southern Fried . 87
    Cacciatore 89
    Casserole 90
    Dad's Marinated 91
    Lemon 90
    My Marinated 91
    Nuggets 88
    Middle East Style . . . 88
    Parmigiana 90
    Strips 88
    Stuffed Breast 89
Chili:
    Con Carne 102
    Hot Dog 102
Cole Slaw:
    Middle East 70
    American 70
Corn Beef Hash 50
Cream Puffs 112

-D-

Dad's Famous Chili 102
Date Cookies 108
Devilled Eggs 57
Dough 78
Dumplings in Yogurt 82

-E-

Easter Cakes
    Middle East 107
Eggplant:
    Parmigiana 60
    Rollatini 59

-F-

Fish:
    With Tahini 57
    Baked 91
    Shrimp Oreganato . . . 92
French Toast 50
Fried Rice 103

-G-

Grape Leaves :
    With Meat 79
    Vegetarian 58

-H-

Ham 96
Hummus 55

-K-

Kefta 80
Kibbee (raw) 58
Kibbee (cooked) 78
Koosa 81

-L-

Lamburgers 80
Lasagna Baked 93
Lentils:
    Soup 64
    and Rice 99
Loobie & Rice 81
Leban 118
Lebanee 118

-M-

Malfoof 82
Mahmool 108
Manicotti 98
Meatless Grape Leaves . . 58
Meat Pies 79
Mfarakee 99
Mjadarah 99

-P-

Pancakes:
    Plain 50
    With Ricotta 109
Swedish 50
Peppers:
    Stuffed 93
    And Sausage 61
Pineapple Upside Down . 113
Pound Cake 114
Pies:
    Crust 114
    Apple 115
    Pumpkin 115
    Pecan 116
Pizza Rustica 94
Potatoes:
    Breakfast Home Fried 74
    Lunch/Dinner
        Home Fried 74
Potato Salad: 74
    Whipped 75
    Potatoes and Eggs . . . 75
    Twice Baked 75
    Warm Potato 76
Potatoes Sweet:
    Candied 76
    Whipped 76
Pot Roast 95
Rice and Noodles 100
Rolled Cabbage 82

-S-

Salads
    Asparagus. 68
    Chicken. 68
    Cucumbers & Yogurt . 72
    Fatoosh 71
    Mixed Salad 71
    Potato 75
    Seven Layer 68
    Tabooli 69
    Tomato & Onion 71
    Shepherd 69
Sausage
    Rolls 61
    And Peppers 92
Sauce Italian 92
Shash Barak 82
Shortbread–Middle East 109
Shrimp:
    Cocktail. 61
    Fried 95
    Oreganato. 92
Soup:
    Chicken
    Rice and Noodles. . . . 64
    Creamed. 64
    Lentil 64
    Split Pea 65
    Vegetable 65

Spareribs Barbequed. . . . 92
Spinach:
    Pies 59
    Sauted. 100
String Beans
    And Rice 81
    And Tomatoes. 100
Stuffed Zucchini. 81
Swedish
    Meatballs 94
    Pancakes. 50
Syrian Cheese 118

-V-

Virginia Ham 96

-Y-

Yogurt:
    Plain. 118
    Yogurt Cheese 118
    With Dumplings. 82

-Z-

Zatar. 62
Ziti Baked. 93
Zucchini:
    Mfaraki. 99
Stuffed 81

My Mother with Lorraine,
George and me (on the left).

My first big "solo" picture.

Left to right: Madlene, Lorraine
and George (you can see why
Lorraine "dominated" us)

The Haddads
Growing up in Clinton, Iowa

My grandfather, Jiddo Sam
(I think he borrowed the
uniform from a soldier)

My grandmother, Sito Takla
(Keeping warm)

My Mother – God Bless Her
(the best cook ever!)

Mom and Dad
Stepping out in New York!

*My Dad – Proud Owner of
Mae Alden's Café in Clinton*

*After a 27 year separation
Mom was reunited with
her mother, Sito Miriam,
during a visit Lebanon*

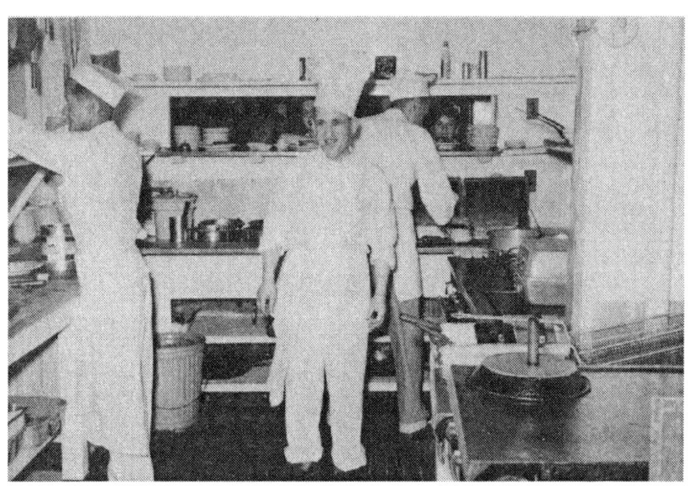

*Dad – The Master Chef in the kitchen at
Mae Alden's Café*

*The Haddad Family at our new house
in Brooklyn New York*

*My children Eddie and
Jeannie as babies.*

*I'm ready to conquer
the business world.*

*An early family get together
(obviously for a meal)
at my parents' home*

The Olson Family – Growing up.

Christmas with Mom

Lorraine, my son Eddie, and me having a good time at (what else) a dinner party.

Lorraine, Mom and me at Lorraine's house

Here I am – a real live Business Executive

*All the brothers and sisters
(and the brothers' spouses)*

*George and Marty come to
New York to celebrate
their wedding in 1973*

*The siblings and spouses
(except George and Marty)
at a family get together.*

*A gathering of the Haddad, Olson,
and Arida Families – circa 1974*

*And then most the cousins
got together (about 20+ years later)*

*Rick, George, Lorraine and I
at my niece's wedding*

All the "older" generation at the wedding

*One of my last pictures with my
dearest sister Lorraine – God Bless her!*